CRIMINAL PROCEDURE

2009 Case and Statutory Supplement

ASPEN PUBLISHERS

CRIMINAL PROCEDURE

2009 Case and Statutory Supplement

Erwin Chemerinsky

Dean and Distinguished Professor of Law
University of California, Irvine, School of Law

Laurie L. Levenson

Professor of Law, William M. Rains Fellow,
and Director, Center for Ethical Advocacy
Loyola Law School

 Wolters Kluwer

Law & Business

AUSTIN   BOSTON   CHICAGO   NEW YORK   THE NETHERLANDS

Aspen Publishers
Attn: Permissions Department
76 Ninth Avenue, 7th Floor
New York, NY 10011-5201

To contact Customer Care, e-mail customer.care@aspenpublishers.com, call 1-800-234-1660, fax 1-800-901-9075, or mail correspondence to:

Aspen Publishers
Attn: Order Department
PO Box 990
Frederick, MD 21705

Printed in the United States of America.

1 2 3 4 5 6 7 8 9 0

ISBN 978-0-7355-8492-1

Library of Congress Cataloging-in-Publication Data

Chemerinsky, Erwin.
  Criminal procedure / Erwin Chemerinsky, Laurie L. Levenson. — 1st ed.
    p. cm.
  Includes index.
  ISBN 978-0-7355-6964-5 (casebook)
  ISBN 978-0-7355-8492-1 (supplement)
  1. Criminal procedure—United States. 2. Due process of law—United States. 3. Criminal procedure—United States—Cases. 4. Due process of law—United States—Cases. I. Levenson, Laurie L., 1956- II. Title.

KF9619.C48 2008
345.73'05—dc22

                                                          2008012664

About Wolters Kluwer Law & Business

Wolters Kluwer Law & Business is a leading provider of research information and workflow solutions in key specialty areas. The strengths of the individual brands of Aspen Publishers, CCH, Kluwer Law International and Loislaw are aligned within Wolters Kluwer Law & Business to provide comprehensive, in-depth solutions and expert-authored content for the legal, professional and education markets.

CCH was founded in 1913 and has served more than four generations of business professionals and their clients. The CCH products in the Wolters Kluwer Law & Business group are highly regarded electronic and print resources for legal, securities, antitrust and trade regulation, government contracting, banking, pension, payroll, employment and labor, and healthcare reimbursement and compliance professionals.

Aspen Publishers is a leading information provider for attorneys, business professionals and law students. Written by preeminent authorities, Aspen products offer analytical and practical information in a range of specialty practice areas from securities law and intellectual property to mergers and acquisitions and pension/benefits. Aspen's trusted legal education resources provide professors and students with high-quality, up-to-date and effective resources for successful instruction and study in all areas of the law.

Kluwer Law International supplies the global business community with comprehensive English-language international legal information. Legal practitioners, corporate counsel and business executives around the world rely on the Kluwer Law International journals, loose-leafs, books and electronic products for authoritative information in many areas of international legal practice.

Loislaw is a premier provider of digitized legal content to small law firm practitioners of various specializations. Loislaw provides attorneys with the ability to quickly and efficiently find the necessary legal information they need, when and where they need it, by facilitating access to primary law as well as state-specific law, records, forms and treatises.

Wolters Kluwer Law & Business, a unit of Wolters Kluwer, is headquartered in New York and Riverwoods, Illinois. Wolters Kluwer is a leading multinational publisher and information services company.

CONTENTS

Contents

PREFACE

Although the casebook was published in 2008 and is current through the end of October Term 2006, which ended on June 28, 2007, this Supplement is needed for two reasons. First, it covers the cases from October Term 2007 and October Term 2008. Second, it is a statutory supplement providing statutory material related to each of the chapters.

We plan to do an annual supplement each year. Each will include the cases since the casebook was published and the most recent version of this statutory material. We welcome comments and suggestions from the professors and students using our book.

Erwin Chemerinsky
Laurie Levenson

August 2009

CRIMINAL PROCEDURE

2009 Case and Statutory Supplement

Chapter 2

SEARCHES AND SEIZURES

E. Exceptions to the Warrant Requirement

4. The Automobile Exception

c. *Searches Incident to Arrest (casebook page 147)*

In *New York v. Belton* (casebook p. 147), the Supreme Court held that the police may search the passenger area of a car and containers within it when a person who has been driving is arrested. In *Arizona v. Gant*, the Court adopts a new rule for situations where the driver and passengers are restrained and do not have access to the car. The police then may search the interior of the car only if they reasonably believe that evidence of the crime that led to the arrest might be found.

Arizona v. Gant
129 S.Ct. 1710 (2009)

Justice STEVENS delivered the opinion of the Court.

After Rodney Gant was arrested for driving with a suspended license, hand-cuffed, and locked in the back of a patrol car, police officers searched his car and discovered cocaine in the pocket of a jacket on the backseat. Because Gant could not have accessed his car to retrieve weapons or evidence at the time of the search, the Arizona Supreme Court held that the search-incident-to-arrest exception to the Fourth Amendment's warrant requirement, as defined in *Chimel v. California* (1969), and applied to vehicle searches in *New York v. Belton* (1981), did not justify the search in this case. We agree with that conclusion.

Under *Chimel*, police may search incident to arrest only the space within an arrestee's "immediate control," meaning "the area from within which he might gain possession of a weapon or destructible evidence." The safety and evidentiary justifications underlying *Chimel's* reaching-distance rule determine *Belton's* scope. Accordingly, we hold that *Belton* does not authorize a vehicle search incident to a recent occupant's arrest after the arrestee has been secured and cannot access the interior of the vehicle. Consistent with the holding in *Thornton v. United States* (2004), we also conclude that circumstances unique to the automobile context justify a search incident to arrest when it is reasonable to believe that evidence of the offense of arrest might be found in the vehicle.

I

On August 25, 1999, acting on an anonymous tip that the residence at 2524 North Walnut Avenue was being used to sell drugs, Tucson police officers Griffith and Reed knocked on the front door and asked to speak to the owner. Gant answered the door and, after identifying himself, stated that he expected the owner to return later. The officers left the residence and conducted a records check, which revealed that Gant's driver's license had been suspended and there was an outstanding warrant for his arrest for driving with a suspended license.

When the officers returned to the house that evening, they found a man near the back of the house and a woman in a car parked in front of it. After a third officer arrived, they arrested the man for providing a false name and the woman for possessing drug paraphernalia. Both arrestees were handcuffed and secured in separate patrol cars when Gant arrived. The officers recognized his car as it entered the driveway, and Officer Griffith confirmed that Gant was the driver by shining a flashlight into the car as it drove by him. Gant parked at the end of the driveway, got out of his car, and shut the door. Griffith, who was about 30 feet away, called to Gant, and they approached each other, meeting 10-to-12 feet from Gant's car. Griffith immediately arrested Gant and handcuffed him.

Because the other arrestees were secured in the only patrol cars at the scene, Griffith called for backup. When two more officers arrived, they locked Gant in the backseat of their vehicle. After Gant had been handcuffed and placed in the back of a patrol car, two officers searched his car: One of them found a gun, and the other discovered a bag of cocaine in the pocket of a jacket on the backseat.

Gant was charged with two offenses—possession of a narcotic drug for sale and possession of drug paraphernalia (*i.e.*, the plastic bag in which the cocaine was found). He moved to suppress the evidence seized from his car on the ground that the warrantless search violated the Fourth Amendment. Among other things, Gant argued that *Belton* did not authorize the search of his vehicle because he posed no threat to the officers after he was handcuffed in the patrol car and because he was arrested for a traffic offense for which no evidence could be found in his vehicle. When asked at the suppression hearing why the search was conducted, Officer Griffith responded: "Because the law says we can do it." The trial court rejected the State's contention that the officers had probable cause to search Gant's car for contraband when the search began, but it denied the motion to suppress. Relying on the fact that the police saw Gant commit the crime of driving without a license and apprehended him only shortly after he exited his car, the court held that the search was permissible as a search incident to arrest. A jury found Gant guilty on both drug counts, and he was sentenced to a 3-year term of imprisonment.

After protracted state-court proceedings, the Arizona Supreme Court concluded that the search of Gant's car was unreasonable within the meaning of the Fourth Amendment. The court's opinion discussed at length our decision in *Belton*, which held that police may search the passenger compartment of a vehicle and any containers therein as a contemporaneous incident of an arrest of the vehicle's recent occupant. The court distinguished *Belton* as a case concerning the permissible scope of a vehicle search incident to arrest and concluded that it did not answer "the threshold question whether the police may conduct a search incident to arrest at all once the scene is secure." When "the justifications underlying *Chimel* no longer exist because the scene is secure and the arrestee is handcuffed, secured in the back of a patrol car, and under the supervision of an officer," the court concluded, a "warrantless search of the arrestee's car cannot be justified as necessary to protect the officers at the scene or prevent the destruction of evidence." Accordingly, the court held that the search of Gant's car was unreasonable.

II

Consistent with our precedent, our analysis begins, as it should in every case addressing the reasonableness of a warrantless search, with the basic rule that "searches conducted outside the judicial process, without prior approval by judge or magistrate, are *per se* unreasonable under the Fourth Amendment— subject only to a few specifically established and well-delineated exceptions." Among the exceptions to the warrant requirement is a search incident to a lawful arrest. The exception derives from interests in officer safety and evidence preservation that are typically implicated in arrest situations.

In *Chimel*, we held that a search incident to arrest may only include "the arrestee's person and the area 'within his immediate control'—construing that phrase to mean the area from within which he might gain possession of a weapon or destructible evidence." That limitation, which continues to define the boundaries of the exception, ensures that the scope of a search incident to arrest is commensurate with its purposes of protecting arresting officers and safeguarding any evidence of the offense of arrest that an arrestee might conceal or destroy. If there is no possibility that an arrestee could reach into the area that law enforcement officers seek to search, both justifications for the search-incident-to-arrest exception are absent and the rule does not apply.

In *Belton*, we considered *Chimel*'s application to the automobile context. A lone police officer in that case stopped a speeding car in which Belton was one of four occupants. While asking for the driver's license and registration, the officer smelled burnt marijuana and observed an envelope on the car floor marked "Supergold"—a name he associated with marijuana. Thus having probable cause to believe the occupants had committed a drug offense, the officer ordered them out of the vehicle, placed them under arrest, and patted them down. Without handcuffing the arrestees, the officer " 'split them up into four separate areas of the Thruway . . . so they would not be in physical touching area of each other' " and searched the vehicle, including the pocket of a jacket on the backseat, in which he found cocaine.

After considering these arguments, we held that when an officer lawfully arrests "the occupant of an automobile, he may, as a contemporaneous incident of that arrest, search the passenger compartment of the automobile" and any containers therein. That holding was based in large part on our assumption "that articles inside the relatively narrow compass of the passenger compartment of an automobile are in fact generally, even if not inevitably, within 'the area into which an arrestee might reach.'"

III

Despite the textual and evidentiary support for the Arizona Supreme Court's reading of *Belton*, our opinion has been widely understood to allow a vehicle search incident to the arrest of a recent occupant even if there is no possibility the arrestee could gain access to the vehicle at the time of the search. Under this broad reading of *Belton*, a vehicle search would be authorized incident to every arrest of a recent occupant notwithstanding that in most cases the vehicle's passenger compartment will not be within the arrestee's reach at the time of the search. To read *Belton* as authorizing a vehicle search incident to every recent occupant's arrest would thus untether the rule from the justifications underlying the *Chimel* exception—a result clearly incompatible with our statement in *Belton* that it "in no way alters the fundamental principles established in the *Chimel* case regarding the basic scope of searches incident to lawful custodial arrests." Accordingly, we reject this reading of *Belton* and hold that the *Chimel* rationale authorizes police to search a vehicle incident to a recent occupant's arrest only when the arrestee is unsecured and within reaching distance of the passenger compartment at the time of the search.

Although it does not follow from *Chimel*, we also conclude that circumstances unique to the vehicle context justify a search incident to a lawful arrest when it is "reasonable to believe evidence relevant to the crime of arrest might be found in the vehicle." In many cases, as when a recent occupant is arrested for a traffic violation, there will be no reasonable basis to believe the vehicle contains relevant evidence. But in others, including *Belton* and *Thornton*, the offense of arrest will supply a basis for searching the passenger compartment of an arrestee's vehicle and any containers therein.

Neither the possibility of access nor the likelihood of discovering offense-related evidence authorized the search in this case. Unlike in *Belton*, which involved a single officer confronted with four unsecured arrestees, the five officers in this case outnumbered the three arrestees, all of whom had been handcuffed and secured in separate patrol cars before the officers searched Gant's car. Under those circumstances, Gant clearly was not within reaching distance of his car at the time of the search. An evidentiary basis for the search was also lacking in this case. Whereas Belton and Thornton were arrested for drug offenses, Gant was arrested for driving with a suspended license—an offense for which police could not expect to find evidence in the passenger compartment of Gant's car. Because police could not reasonably have believed either that Gant could have accessed his car at the time of the search or that evidence of the offense for which he was arrested might have been found therein, the search in this case was unreasonable.

4

IV

The State does not seriously disagree with the Arizona Supreme Court's conclusion that Gant could not have accessed his vehicle at the time of the search, but it nevertheless asks us to uphold the search of his vehicle under the broad reading of *Belton* discussed above. The State argues that *Belton* searches are reasonable regardless of the possibility of access in a given case because that expansive rule correctly balances law enforcement interests, including the interest in a bright-line rule, with an arrestee's limited privacy interest in his vehicle.

For several reasons, we reject the State's argument. First, the State seriously undervalues the privacy interests at stake. Although we have recognized that a motorist's privacy interest in his vehicle is less substantial than in his home, the former interest is nevertheless important and deserving of constitutional protection. It is particularly significant that *Belton* searches authorize police officers to search not just the passenger compartment but every purse, briefcase, or other container within that space. A rule that gives police the power to conduct such a search whenever an individual is caught committing a traffic offense, when there is no basis for believing evidence of the offense might be found in the vehicle, creates a serious and recurring threat to the privacy of countless individuals. Indeed, the character of that threat implicates the central concern underlying the Fourth Amendment—the concern about giving police officers unbridled discretion to rummage at will among a person's private effects.

At the same time as it undervalues these privacy concerns, the State exaggerates the clarity that its reading of *Belton* provides. Courts that have read *Belton* expansively are at odds regarding how close in time to the arrest and how proximate to the arrestee's vehicle an officer's first contact with the arrestee must be to bring the encounter within *Belton*'s purview and whether a search is reasonable when it commences or continues after the arrestee has been removed from the scene. The rule has thus generated a great deal of uncertainty, particularly for a rule touted as providing a "bright line."

Contrary to the State's suggestion, a broad reading of *Belton* is also unnecessary to protect law enforcement safety and evidentiary interests. Under our view, *Belton* and *Thornton* permit an officer to conduct a vehicle search when an arrestee is within reaching distance of the vehicle or it is reasonable to believe the vehicle contains evidence of the offense of arrest. Other established exceptions to the warrant requirement authorize a vehicle search under additional circumstances when safety or evidentiary concerns demand.

These exceptions together ensure that officers may search a vehicle when genuine safety or evidentiary concerns encountered during the arrest of a vehicle's recent occupant justify a search. Construing *Belton* broadly to allow vehicle searches incident to any arrest would serve no purpose except to provide a police entitlement, and it is anathema to the Fourth Amendment to permit a warrantless search on that basis. For these reasons, we are unpersuaded by the State's arguments that a broad reading of *Belton* would meaningfully further law enforcement interests and justify a substantial intrusion on individuals' privacy.

V

Our dissenting colleagues argue that the doctrine of *stare decisis* requires adherence to a broad reading of *Belton* even though the justifications for searching a vehicle incident to arrest are in most cases absent. The doctrine of *stare decisis* is of course "essential to the respect accorded to the judgments of the Court and to the stability of the law," but it does not compel us to follow a past decision when its rationale no longer withstands "careful analysis."

We have never relied on *stare decisis* to justify the continuance of an unconstitutional police practice. And we would be particularly loath to uphold an unconstitutional result in a case that is so easily distinguished from the decisions that arguably compel it. The safety and evidentiary interests that supported the search in *Belton* simply are not present in this case. Indeed, it is hard to imagine two cases that are factually more distinct, as *Belton* involved one officer confronted by four unsecured arrestees suspected of committing a drug offense and this case involves several officers confronted with a securely detained arrestee apprehended for driving with a suspended license. This case is also distinguishable from *Thornton*, in which the petitioner was arrested for a drug offense. It is thus unsurprising that Members of this Court who concurred in the judgments in *Belton* and *Thornton* also concur in the decision in this case.

VI

Police may search a vehicle incident to a recent occupant's arrest only if the arrestee is within reaching distance of the passenger compartment at the time of the search or it is reasonable to believe the vehicle contains evidence of the offense of arrest. When these justifications are absent, a search of an arrestee's vehicle will be unreasonable unless police obtain a warrant or show that another exception to the warrant requirement applies.

Justice SCALIA, concurring.

To determine what is an "unreasonable" search within the meaning of the Fourth Amendment, we look first to the historical practices the Framers sought to preserve; if those provide inadequate guidance, we apply traditional standards of reasonableness. Since the historical scope of officers' authority to search vehicles incident to arrest is uncertain, traditional standards of reasonableness govern. It is abundantly clear that those standards do not justify what I take to be the rule set forth in *New York v. Belton* (1981), that arresting officers may always search an arrestee's vehicle in order to protect themselves from hidden weapons. When an arrest is made in connection with a roadside stop, police virtually always have a less intrusive and more effective means of ensuring their safety—and a means that is virtually always employed: ordering the arrestee away from the vehicle, patting him down in the open, handcuffing him, and placing him in the squad car.

Law enforcement officers face a risk of being shot whenever they pull a car over. But that risk is at its height at the time of the initial confrontation; and it is *not at all* reduced by allowing a search of the stopped vehicle after the driver has been arrested and placed in the squad car. I observed in *Thornton* that the government had failed to provide a single instance in which a formerly restrained arrestee escaped to retrieve a weapon from his own vehicle; Arizona and its *amici* have not remedied that significant deficiency in the present case.

It must be borne in mind that we are speaking here only of a rule automatically permitting a search when the driver or an occupant is arrested. Where no arrest is made, we have held that officers may search the car if they reasonably believe "the suspect is dangerous and . . . may gain immediate control of weapons." In the no-arrest case, the possibility of access to weapons in the vehicle always exists, since the driver or passenger will be allowed to return to the vehicle when the interrogation is completed. The rule of *Michigan v. Long* is not at issue here.

Justice STEVENS acknowledges that an officer-safety rationale cannot justify all vehicle searches incident to arrest, but asserts that that is not the rule *Belton* and *Thornton* adopted. Justice STEVENS would therefore retain the application of *Chimel v. California* (1969), in the car-search context but would apply in the future what he believes our cases held in the past: that officers making a roadside stop may search the vehicle so long as the "arrestee is within reaching distance of the passenger compartment at the time of the search." I believe that this standard fails to provide the needed guidance to arresting officers and also leaves much room for manipulation, inviting officers to leave the scene unsecured (at least where dangerous suspects are not involved) in order to conduct a vehicle search. In my view we should simply abandon the *Belton-Thornton* charade of officer safety and overrule those cases. I would hold that a vehicle search incident to arrest is *ipso facto* "reasonable" only when the object of the search is evidence of the crime for which the arrest was made, or of another crime that the officer has probable cause to believe occurred. Because respondent was arrested for driving without a license (a crime for which no evidence could be expected to be found in the vehicle), I would hold in the present case that the search was unlawful.

Justice ALITO insists that the Court must demand a good reason for abandoning prior precedent. That is true enough, but it seems to me ample reason that the precedent was badly reasoned and produces erroneous (in this case unconstitutional) results.

No other Justice, however, shares my view that application of *Chimel* in this context should be entirely abandoned. It seems to me unacceptable for the Court to come forth with a 4-to-1-to-4 opinion that leaves the governing rule uncertain. I am therefore confronted with the choice of either leaving the current understanding of *Belton* and *Thornton* in effect, or acceding to what seems to me the artificial narrowing of those cases adopted by Justice STEVENS. The latter, as I have said, does not provide the degree of certainty I think desirable in this field; but the former opens the field to what I think are plainly unconstitutional searches—which is the greater evil. I therefore join the opinion of the Court.

Justice ALITO, with whom THE CHIEF JUSTICE and Justice KENNEDY join, and with whom Justice BREYER joins except as to Part II-E, dissenting.

Twenty-eight years ago, in *New York v. Belton* (1981), this Court held that "when a policeman has made a lawful custodial arrest of the occupant of an automobile, he may, as a contemporaneous incident of that arrest, search the passenger compartment of that automobile." Five years ago, in *Thornton v. United States* (2004)—a case involving a situation not materially distinguishable from the situation here—the Court not only reaffirmed but extended the holding of *Belton*, making it applicable to recent occupants. Today's decision effectively overrules those important decisions, even though respondent Gant has not asked us to do so.

To take the place of the overruled precedents, the Court adopts a new two-part rule under which a police officer who arrests a vehicle occupant or recent occupant may search the passenger compartment if (1) the arrestee is within reaching distance of the vehicle at the time of the search or (2) the officer has reason to believe that the vehicle contains evidence of the offense of arrest. The first part of this new rule may endanger arresting officers and is truly endorsed by only four Justices; Justice SCALIA joins solely for the purpose of avoiding a "4-to-1-to-4 opinion." The second part of the new rule is taken from Justice SCALIA's separate opinion in *Thornton* without any independent explanation of its origin or justification and is virtually certain to confuse law enforcement officers and judges for some time to come. The Court's decision will cause the suppression of evidence gathered in many searches carried out in good-faith reliance on well-settled case law, and although the Court purports to base its analysis on the land-mark decision in *Chimel v. California* (1969), the Court's reasoning undermines *Chimel*. I would follow *Belton*, and I therefore respectfully dissent.

I

Although the Court refuses to acknowledge that it is overruling *Belton* and *Thornton*, there can be no doubt that it does so. The precise holding in *Belton* could not be clearer. The Court stated unequivocally: "[W]e hold that when a policeman has made a lawful custodial arrest of the occupant of an automobile, he may, as a contemporaneous incident of that arrest, search the passenger compartment of that automobile."

Despite this explicit statement, the opinion of the Court in the present case curiously suggests that *Belton* may reasonably be read as adopting a holding that is narrower than the one explicitly set out in the *Belton* opinion, namely, that an officer arresting a vehicle occupant may search the passenger compartment "*when the passenger compartment is within an arrestee's reaching distance.*"

II

Because the Court has substantially overruled *Belton* and *Thornton*, the Court must explain why its departure from the usual rule of *stare decisis* is justified.

I recognize that stare decisis is not an "inexorable command," and applies less rigidly in constitutional cases. But the Court has said that a constitutional precedent should be followed unless there is a "special justification" for its abandonment. Relevant factors identified in prior cases include whether the precedent has engendered reliance, whether there has been an important change in circumstances in the outside world, whether the precedent has proved to be unworkable, whether the precedent has been undermined by later decisions, and whether the decision was badly reasoned. These factors weigh in favor of retaining the rule established in *Belton*.

A

Reliance. While reliance is most important in "cases involving property and contract rights," the Court has recognized that reliance by law enforcement officers is also entitled to weight. [T]here certainly is substantial reliance here. The *Belton* rule has been taught to police officers for more than a quarter century. Many searches—almost certainly including more than a few that figure in cases now on appeal—were conducted in scrupulous reliance on that precedent. It is likely that, on the very day when this opinion is announced, numerous vehicle searches will be conducted in good faith by police officers who were taught the *Belton* rule.

B

Changed circumstances. Abandonment of the *Belton* rule cannot be justified on the ground that the dangers surrounding the arrest of a vehicle occupant are different today than they were 28 years ago.

C

Workability. The *Belton* rule has not proved to be unworkable. On the contrary, the rule was adopted for the express purpose of providing a test that would be relatively easy for police officers and judges to apply. The Court correctly notes that even the *Belton* rule is not perfectly clear in all situations. Specifically, it is sometimes debatable whether a search is or is not contemporaneous with an arrest, but that problem is small in comparison with the problems that the Court's new two-part rule will produce.

D

Consistency with later cases. The *Belton* bright-line rule has not been undermined by subsequent cases. On the contrary, that rule was reaffirmed and extended just five years ago in *Thornton*.

E

Bad reasoning. The Court is harshly critical of *Belton*'s reasoning, but the problem that the Court perceives cannot be remedied simply by overruling *Belton*. *Belton* represented only a modest—and quite defensible—extension of *Chimel*, as I understand that decision.

F

The Court, however, does not reexamine *Chimel* and thus leaves the law relating to searches incident to arrest in a confused and unstable state. The first part of the Court's new two-part rule—which permits an arresting officer to search the area within an arrestee's reach at the time of the search—applies, at least for now, only to vehicle occupants and recent occupants, but there is no logical reason why the same rule should not apply to all arrestees.

The second part of the Court's new rule, which the Court takes uncritically from Justice SCALIA's separate opinion in *Thornton*, raises doctrinal and practical problems that the Court makes no effort to address. Why, for example, is the standard for this type of evidence-gathering search "reason to believe" rather than probable cause? And why is this type of search restricted to evidence of the offense of arrest? It is true that an arrestee's vehicle is probably more likely to contain evidence of the crime of arrest than of some other crime, but if reason-to-believe is the governing standard for an evidence-gathering search incident to arrest, it is not easy to see why an officer should not be able to search when the officer has reason to believe that the vehicle in question possesses evidence of a crime other than the crime of arrest.

Nor is it easy to see why an evidence-gathering search incident to arrest should be restricted to the passenger compartment. The *Belton* rule was limited in this way because the passenger compartment was considered to be the area that vehicle occupants can generally reach but since the second part of the new rule is not based on officer safety or the preservation of evidence, the ground for this limitation is obscure.

III

Respondent in this case has not asked us to overrule *Belton*, much less *Chimel*. Respondent's argument rests entirely on an interpretation of *Belton* that is plainly incorrect, an interpretation that disregards *Belton*'s explicit delineation of its holding. I would therefore leave any reexamination of our prior precedents for another day, if such a reexamination is to be undertaken at all. In this case, I would simply apply *Belton* and reverse the judgment below.

10. Searches When There Are Special Needs

b. Schools *(casebook page 200)*

In *New Jersey v. TLO* (casebook, p. 200), the Supreme Court held that students' possessions may be searched in schools if there is reasonable suspicion that they have evidence of illegal activity. In *Safford Unified School District v. Redding*, the Court considered the circumstances under which a student may be subjected to a strip search.

and underpants by Romero and Schwallier, as Savana was later on. The search revealed no additional pills.

It was at this juncture that Wilson called Savana into his office and showed her the day planner. Their conversation established that Savana and Marissa were on friendly terms: while she denied knowledge of the contraband, Savana admitted that the day planner was hers and that she had lent it to Marissa. Wilson had other reports of their friendship from staff members, who had identified Savana and Marissa as part of an unusually rowdy group at the school's opening dance in August, during which alcohol and cigarettes were found in the girls' bathroom. Wilson had reason to connect the girls with this contraband, for Wilson knew that Jordan Romero had told the principal that before the dance, he had been at a party at Savana's house where alcohol was served. Marissa's statement that the pills came from Savana was thus sufficiently plausible to warrant suspicion that Savana was involved in pill distribution.

This suspicion of Wilson's was enough to justify a search of Savana's back-pack and outer clothing. If a student is reasonably suspected of giving out contra-band pills, she is reasonably suspected of carrying them on her person and in the carryall that has become an item of student uniform in most places today. If Wilson's reasonable suspicion of pill distribution were not understood to support searches of outer clothes and backpack, it would not justify any search worth making. And the look into Savana's bag, in her presence and in the relative privacy of Wilson's office, was not excessively intrusive, any more than Romero's subse-quent search of her outer clothing.

B

Here it is that the parties part company, with Savana's claim that extending the search at Wilson's behest to the point of making her pull out her underwear was constitutionally unreasonable. The exact label for this final step in the intru-sion is not important, though strip search is a fair way to speak of it. Romero and Schwallier directed Savana to remove her clothes down to her underwear, and then "pull out" her bra and the elastic band on her underpants. Although Romero and Schwallier stated that they did not see anything when Savana followed their instructions, we would not define strip search and its Fourth Amendment con-sequences in a way that would guarantee litigation about who was looking and how much was seen. The very fact of Savana's pulling her underwear away from her body in the presence of the two officials who were able to see her necessarily exposed her breasts and pelvic area to some degree, and both subjective and reasonable societal expectations of personal privacy support the treatment of such a search as categorically distinct, requiring distinct elements of justification on the part of school authorities for going beyond a search of outer clothing and belongings.

Savana's subjective expectation of privacy against such a search is inherent in her account of it as embarrassing, frightening, and humiliating. The reasonable-ness of her expectation (required by the Fourth Amendment standard) is indicated by the consistent experiences of other young people similarly searched, whose adolescent vulnerability intensifies the patent intrusiveness of the exposure. The common reaction of these adolescents simply registers the obviously different meaning of a search exposing the body from the experience of nakedness or near undress in other school circumstances. Changing for gym is getting ready for play; exposing for a search is responding to an accusation reserved for suspected wrongdoers and fairly understood as so degrading that a number of communities have decided that strip searches in schools are never reasonable and have banned them no matter what the facts may be.

The indignity of the search does not, of course, outlaw it, but it does implicate the rule of reasonableness as stated in *T.L.O.*, that "the search as actually conducted [be] reasonably related in scope to the circumstances which justified the interference in the first place." The scope will be permissible, that is, when it is "not excessively intrusive in light of the age and sex of the student and the nature of the infraction."

Here, the content of the suspicion failed to match the degree of intrusion. Wilson knew beforehand that the pills were prescription-strength ibuprofen and over-the-counter naproxen, common pain relievers equivalent to two Advil, or one Aleve. He must have been aware of the nature and limited threat of the specific drugs he was searching for, and while just about anything can be taken in quantities that will do real harm, Wilson had no reason to suspect that large amounts of the drugs were being passed around, or that individual students were receiving great numbers of pills.

Nor could Wilson have suspected that Savana was hiding common painkillers in her underwear. Petitioners suggest, as a truth universally acknowledged, that "students ... hid[e] contraband in or under their clothing," and cite a smattering of cases of students with contraband in their underwear. But when the categorically extreme intrusiveness of a search down to the body of an adolescent requires some justification in suspected facts, general background possibilities fall short; a reasonable search that extensive calls for suspicion that it will pay off. But nondangerous school contraband does not raise the specter of stashes in intimate places, and there is no evidence in the record of any general practice among Safford Middle School students of hiding that sort of thing in underwear; neither Jordan nor Marissa suggested to Wilson that Savana was doing that, and the preceding search of Marissa that Wilson ordered yielded nothing. Wilson never even determined when Marissa had received the pills from Savana; if it had been a few days before, that would weigh heavily against any reasonable conclusion that Savana presently had the pills on her person, much less in her underwear.

In sum, what was missing from the suspected facts that pointed to Savana was any indication of danger to the students from the power of the drugs or their quantity, and any reason to suppose that Savana was carrying pills in her underwear. We think that the combination of these deficiencies was fatal to finding the search reasonable.

In so holding, we mean to cast no ill reflection on the assistant principal, for the record raises no doubt that his motive throughout was to eliminate drugs from his school and protect students from what Jordan Romero had gone through. Parents are known to overreact to protect their children from danger, and a school official with responsibility for safety may tend to do the same. The difference is that the Fourth Amendment places limits on the official, even with the high degree of deference that courts must pay to the educator's professional judgment.

We do mean, though, to make it clear that the *T.L.O.* concern to limit a school search to reasonable scope requires the support of reasonable suspicion of danger or of resort to underwear for hiding evidence of wrongdoing before a search can reasonably make the quantum leap from outer clothes and backpacks to exposure of intimate parts. The meaning of such a search, and the degradation its subject may reasonably feel, place a search that intrusive in a category of its own demanding its own specific suspicions.

IV

[The Court then held that the school officials could not be held liable for money damages because they were protected by qualified immunity; that is, they did not violate clearly established law that the reasonable officer should know. The Court remanded the case to determine if the school district could be held liable for a policy that violated the Fourth Amendment.]

Justice THOMAS, concurring in the judgment in part and dissenting in part.

I agree with the Court that the judgment against the school officials with respect to qualified immunity should be reversed. Unlike the majority, however, I would hold that the search of Savana Redding did not violate the Fourth Amendment. The majority imposes a vague and amorphous standard on school administrators. It also grants judges sweeping authority to second-guess the measures that these officials take to maintain discipline in their schools and ensure the health and safety of the students in their charge. This deep intrusion into the administration of public schools exemplifies why the Court should return to the common-law doctrine of *in loco parentis* under which "the judiciary was reluctant to interfere in the routine business of school administration, allowing schools and teachers to set and enforce rules and to maintain order." But even under the prevailing Fourth Amendment test established by *New Jersey v. T.L.O.*, 469 U.S. 325, 105 S.Ct. 733, 83 L.Ed.2d 720 (1985), all petitioners, including the school district, are entitled to judgment as a matter of law in their favor.

I

"Although the underlying command of the Fourth Amendment is always that searches and seizures be reasonable, what is reasonable depends on the context within which a search takes place." Thus, although public school students retain

Fourth Amendment rights under this Court's precedent, those rights "are different . . . than elsewhere; the 'reasonableness' inquiry cannot disregard the schools' custodial and tutelary responsibility for children." For nearly 25 years this Court has understood that "[m]aintaining order in the classroom has never been easy, but in more recent years, school disorder has often taken particularly ugly forms: drug use and violent crime in the schools have become major social problems." In schools, "[e]vents calling for discipline are frequent occurrences and sometimes require immediate, effective action."

For this reason, school officials retain broad authority to protect students and preserve "order and a proper educational environment" under the Fourth Amendment. This authority requires that school officials be able to engage in the "close supervision of schoolchildren, as well as . . . enforc[e] rules against conduct that would be perfectly permissible if undertaken by an adult." Seeking to reconcile the Fourth Amendment with this unique public school setting, the Court in *T.L.O.* held that a school search is "reasonable" if it is " 'justified at its inception' " and " 'reasonably related in scope to the circumstances which justified the interference in the first place.' " The search under review easily meets this standard.

A

A "search of a student by a teacher or other school official will be 'justified at its inception' when there are reasonable grounds for suspecting that the search will turn up evidence that the student has violated or is violating either the law or the rules of the school." As the majority rightly concedes, this search was justified at its inception because there were reasonable grounds to suspect that Redding possessed medication that violated school rules.

B

The remaining question is whether the search was reasonable in scope. Under *T.L.O.*, "a search will be permissible in its scope when the measures adopted are reasonably related to the objectives of the search and not excessively intrusive in light of the age and sex of the student and the nature of the infraction." The majority concludes that the school officials' search of Redding's underwear was not "reasonably related in scope to the circumstances which justified the interference in the first place," notwithstanding the officials' reasonable suspicion that Redding "was involved in pill distribution." According to the majority, to be reasonable, this school search required a showing of "danger to the students from the power of the drugs or their quantity" or a "reason to suppose that [Redding] was carrying pills in her underwear." Each of these additional requirements is an unjustifiable departure from bedrock Fourth Amendment law in the school setting, where this Court has heretofore read the Fourth Amendment to grant considerable leeway to school officials. Because the school officials searched in a location where the pills could have been hidden, the search was reasonable in scope under *T.L.O.*

Searches and Seizures

1

The majority finds that "subjective and reasonable societal expectations of personal privacy support ... treat[ing]" this type of search, which it labels a "strip search," as "categorically distinct, requiring distinct elements of justification on the part of school authorities for going beyond a search of clothing and belongings." Thus, in the majority's view, although the school officials had reasonable suspicion to believe that Redding had the pills on her person, they needed some greater level of particularized suspicion to conduct this "strip search." There is no support for this contortion of the Fourth Amendment.

The Court has generally held that the reasonableness of a search's scope depends only on whether it is limited to the area that is capable of concealing the object of the search. In keeping with this longstanding rule, the "nature of the infraction" referenced in *T.L.O.* delineates the proper scope of a search of students in a way that is identical to that permitted for searches outside the school—*i.e.*, the search must be limited to the areas where the object of that infraction could be concealed. A search of a student therefore is permissible in scope under *T.L.O.* so long as it is objectively reasonable to believe that the area searched could conceal the contraband.

The analysis of whether the scope of the search here was permissible under that standard is straightforward. Indeed, the majority does not dispute that "general background possibilities" establish that students conceal "contraband in their underwear." It acknowledges that school officials had reasonable suspicion to look in Redding's backpack and outer clothing because if "Wilson's reasonable suspicion of pill distribution were not understood to support searches of outer clothes and backpack, it would not justify any search worth making." The majority nevertheless concludes that proceeding any further with the search was unreasonable. But there is no support for this conclusion. The reasonable suspicion that Redding possessed the pills for distribution purposes did not dissipate simply because the search of her backpack turned up nothing. It was eminently reasonable to conclude that the backpack was empty because Redding was secreting the pills in a place she thought no one would look. Redding would not have been the first person to conceal pills in her undergarments.

2

The majority's decision in this regard also departs from another basic principle of the Fourth Amendment: that law enforcement officials can enforce with the same vigor all rules and regulations irrespective of the perceived importance of any of those rules. "In a long line of cases, we have said that when an officer has probable cause to believe a person committed even a minor crime in his presence, the balancing of private and public interests is not in doubt. The arrest is constitutionally reasonable." The Fourth Amendment rule for searches is the same: Police officers are entitled to search regardless of the perceived triviality of the underlying law. As we have explained, requiring police to make "sensitive, case-by-case determinations of government need," for a particular prohibition before conducting a search would "place police in an almost impossible spot."

The majority has placed school officials in this "impossible spot" by questioning whether possession of Ibuprofen and Naproxen causes a severe enough threat to warrant investigation. Had the suspected infraction involved a street drug, the majority implies that it would have approved the scope of the search. In effect, then, the majority has replaced a school rule that draws no distinction among drugs with a new one that does. As a result, a full search of a student's person for prohibited drugs will be permitted only if the Court agrees that the drug in question was sufficiently dangerous. Such a test is unworkable and unsound. School officials cannot be expected to halt searches based on the possibility that a court might later find that the particular infraction at issue is not severe enough to warrant an intrusive investigation.

A rule promulgated by a school board represents the judgment of school officials that the rule is needed to maintain "school order" and "a proper educational environment." Teachers, administrators, and the local school board are called upon both to "protect the . . . safety of students and school personnel" and "maintain an environment conducive to learning." They are tasked with "watch[ing] over a large number of students" who "are inclined to test the outer boundaries of acceptable conduct and to imitate the misbehavior of a peer if that misbehavior is not dealt with quickly." In such an environment, something as simple as a "water pistol or peashooter can wreak [havoc] until it is taken away." The danger posed by unchecked distribution and consumption of prescription pills by students certainly needs no elaboration.

Judges are not qualified to second-guess the best manner for maintaining quiet and order in the school environment. Such institutional judgments, like those concerning the selection of the best methods for "restrain[ing students] from assaulting one another, abusing drugs and alcohol, and committing other crimes," "involve a host of policy choices that must be made by locally elected representatives, rather than by federal judges interpreting the basic charter of Government for the entire country."

3

Even if this Court were authorized to second-guess the importance of school rules, the Court's assessment of the importance of this district's policy is flawed. It is a crime to possess or use prescription-strength Ibuprofen without a prescription. By prohibiting unauthorized prescription drugs on school grounds—and conducting a search to ensure students abide by that prohibition—the school rule here was consistent with a routine provision of the state criminal code. It hardly seems unreasonable for school officials to enforce a rule that, in effect, proscribes conduct that amounts to a crime. Moreover, school districts have valid reasons for punishing the unauthorized possession of prescription drugs on school property as severely as the possession of street drugs; "[t]eenage abuse of over-the-counter and prescription drugs poses an increasingly alarming national crisis." As one study noted, "more young people ages 12-17 abuse prescription drugs than any illicit drug except marijuana—more than cocaine, heroin, and methamphetamine combined."

In determining whether the search's scope was reasonable under the Fourth Amendment, it is therefore irrelevant whether officials suspected Redding of possessing prescription-strength Ibuprofen, nonprescription-strength Naproxen, or some harder street drug. Safford prohibited its possession on school property. Reasonable suspicion that Redding was in possession of drugs in violation of these policies, therefore, justified a search extending to any area where small pills could be concealed. The search did not violate the Fourth Amendment.

II

By declaring the search unreasonable in this case, the majority has "surrender[ed] control of the American public school system to public school students" by invalidating school policies that treat all drugs equally and by second-guessing swift disciplinary decisions made by school officials. The Court's interference in these matters of great concern to teachers, parents, and students illustrates why the most constitutionally sound approach to the question of applying the Fourth Amendment in local public schools would in fact be the complete restoration of the common-law doctrine of *in loco parentis*.

"[T]he nationwide drug epidemic makes the war against drugs a pressing concern in every school." And yet the Court has limited the authority of school officials to conduct searches for the drugs that the officials believe pose a serious safety risk to their students. By doing so, the majority has confirmed that a return to the doctrine of *in loco parentis* is required to keep the judiciary from essentially seizing control of public schools. Only then will teachers again be able to "govern the[ir] pupils, quicken the slothful, spur the indolent, restrain the impetuous, and control the stubborn" by making "rules, giv[ing] commands, and punish[ing] disobedience" without interference from judges. By deciding that it is better equipped to decide what behavior should be permitted in schools, the Court has undercut student safety and undermined the authority of school administrators and local officials. Even more troubling, it has done so in a case in which the underlying response by school administrators was reasonable and justified. I cannot join this regrettable decision.

F.   Seizures and Arrests

3.   For What Crimes May a Person Be Arrested?
(casebook, p. 239)

In *Atwater v. City of Lago Vista* (casebook, p. 239), the Supreme Court held that there can be custodial arrests even for traffic violations so long as there is probable cause that a crime has been committed. An issue left open in *Atwater* is whether such arrests are permissible if they violate *state* law. That is the question decided in *Virginia v. Moore*.

Virginia v. Moore
128 S.Ct. 1598 (2008)

Justice SCALIA delivered the opinion of the Court.

We consider whether a police officer violates the Fourth Amendment by making an arrest based on probable cause but prohibited by state law.

I

On February 20, 2003, two City of Portsmouth police officers stopped a car driven by David Lee Moore. They had heard over the police radio that a person known as "Chubs" was driving with a suspended license, and one of the officers knew Moore by that nickname. The officers determined that Moore's license was in fact suspended, and arrested him for the misdemeanor of driving on a suspended license, which is punishable under Virginia law by a year in jail and a $2,500 fine, The officers subsequently searched Moore and found that he was carrying 16 grams of crack cocaine and $516 in cash.

Under state law, the officers should have issued Moore a summons instead of arresting him. Driving on a suspended license, like some other misdemeanors, is not an arrestable offense except as to those who "fail or refuse to discontinue" the violation, and those whom the officer reasonably believes to be likely to disregard a summons, or likely to harm themselves or others. The intermediate appellate court found none of these circumstances applicable, and Virginia did not appeal that determination. Virginia also permits arrest for driving on a suspended license in jurisdictions where "prior general approval has been granted by order of the general district court"; Virginia has never claimed such approval was in effect in the county where Moore was arrested.

Moore was charged with possessing cocaine with the intent to distribute it in violation of Virginia law. He filed a pretrial motion to suppress the evidence from the arrest search. Virginia law does not, as a general matter, require suppression of evidence obtained in violation of state law. Moore argued, however, that suppression was required by the Fourth Amendment. The trial court denied the motion, and after a bench trial found Moore guilty of the drug charge and sentenced him to a 5-year prison term, with one year and six months of the sentence suspended. The conviction was reversed by a panel of Virginia's intermediate court on Fourth Amendment grounds, reinstated by the intermediate court sitting en banc, and finally reversed again by the Virginia Supreme Court. The Court reasoned that since the arresting officers should have issued Moore a citation under state law, and the Fourth Amendment does not permit search incident to citation, the arrest search violated the Fourth Amendment.

II

The Fourth Amendment protects "against unreasonable searches and seizures" of (among other things) the person. In determining whether a search or seizure is unreasonable, we begin with history. We look to the statutes and common law of the founding era to determine the norms that the Fourth Amendment was meant to preserve.

We are aware of no historical indication that those who ratified the Fourth Amendment understood it as a redundant guarantee of whatever limits on search and seizure legislatures might have enacted. The immediate object of the Fourth Amendment was to prohibit the general warrants and writs of assistance that English judges had employed against the colonists. That suggests, if anything, that founding-era citizens were skeptical of using the rules for search and seizure set by government actors as the index of reasonableness.

Of course such a claim would not have been available against state officers, since the Fourth Amendment was a restriction only upon federal power. But early Congresses tied the arrest authority of federal officers to state laws of arrest. Moreover, even though several state constitutions also prohibited unreasonable searches and seizures, citizens who claimed officers had violated state restrictions on arrest did not claim that the violations also ran afoul of the state constitutions. The apparent absence of such litigation is particularly striking in light of the fact that searches incident to warrantless arrests (which is to say arrests in which the officer was not insulated from private suit) were, as one commentator has put it, "taken for granted" at the founding, as were warrantless arrests themselves.

III

When history has not provided a conclusive answer, we have analyzed a search or seizure in light of traditional standards of reasonableness "by assessing, on the one hand, the degree to which it intrudes upon an individual's privacy and, on the other, the degree to which it is needed for the promotion of legitimate governmental interests." That methodology provides no support for Moore's Fourth Amendment claim. In a long line of cases, we have said that when an officer has probable cause to believe a person committed even a minor crime in his presence, the balancing of private and public interests is not in doubt. The arrest is constitutionally reasonable.

Our decisions counsel against changing this calculus when a State chooses to protect privacy beyond the level that the Fourth Amendment requires. We have treated additional protections exclusively as matters of state law.

We are convinced that the approach of our prior cases is correct, because an arrest based on probable cause serves interests that have long been seen as sufficient to justify the seizure. Arrest ensures that a suspect appears to answer charges and does not continue a crime, and it safeguards evidence and enables officers to conduct an in-custody investigation.

Moore argues that a State has no interest in arrest when it has a policy against arresting for certain crimes. That is not so, because arrest will still ensure a suspect's appearance at trial, prevent him from continuing his offense, and enable officers to investigate the incident more thoroughly. State arrest restrictions are more accurately characterized as showing that the State values its interests in forgoing arrests more highly than its interests in making them. A State is free to prefer one search-and-seizure policy among the range of constitutionally permissible options, but its choice of a more restrictive option does not render the less restrictive ones unreasonable, and hence unconstitutional.

If we concluded otherwise, we would often frustrate rather than further state policy. Virginia chooses to protect individual privacy and dignity more than the Fourth Amendment requires, but it also chooses not to attach to violations of its arrest rules the potent remedies that federal courts have applied to Fourth Amendment violations. Virginia does not, for example, ordinarily exclude from criminal trials evidence obtained in violation of its statutes. Moore would allow Virginia to accord enhanced protection against arrest only on pain of accompanying that protection with federal remedies for Fourth Amendment violations, which often include the exclusionary rule. States unwilling to lose control over the remedy would have to abandon restrictions on arrest altogether. This is an odd consequence of a provision designed to protect against searches and seizures.

Even if we thought that state law changed the nature of the Commonwealth's interests for purposes of the Fourth Amendment, we would adhere to the probable-cause standard. In determining what is reasonable under the Fourth Amendment, we have given great weight to the "essential interest in readily administrable rules." In Atwater [v. City of Lago Vista (2001)], we acknowledged that nuanced judgments about the need for warrantless arrest were desirable, but we nonetheless declined to limit to felonies and disturbances of the peace the Fourth Amendment rule allowing arrest based on probable cause to believe a law has been broken in the presence of the arresting officer. The rule extends even to minor misdemeanors, we concluded, because of the need for a bright-line constitutional standard. If the constitutionality of arrest for minor offenses turned in part on inquiries as to risk of flight and danger of repetition, officers might be deterred from making legitimate arrests. We found little to justify this cost, because there was no "epidemic of unnecessary minor-offense arrests," and hence "a dearth of horribles demanding redress."

Incorporating state-law arrest limitations into the Constitution would produce a constitutional regime no less vague and unpredictable than the one we rejected in Atwater. The constitutional standard would be only as easy to apply as the underlying state law, and state law can be complicated indeed. The Virginia statute in this case, for example, calls on law enforcement officers to weigh just the sort of case-specific factors that Atwater said would deter legitimate arrests if made part of the constitutional inquiry. It would authorize arrest if a misdemeanor suspect fails or refuses to discontinue the unlawful act, or if the officer believes the suspect to be likely to disregard a summons. Atwater specifically noted the "extremely poor judgment" displayed in arresting a local resident who would "almost certainly" have discontinued the offense and who had "no place to hide and no incentive to flee." It nonetheless declined to make those considerations part of the constitutional calculus. Atwater differs from this case in only one significant respect: It considered (and rejected) federal constitutional remedies for all minor-misdemeanor arrests; Moore seeks them in only that subset of minor-misdemeanor arrests in which there is the least to be gained-that is, where the State has already acted to constrain officers' discretion and prevent abuse. Here we confront fewer horribles than in Atwater, and less of a need for redress.

Finally, linking Fourth Amendment protections to state law would cause them to "vary from place to place and from time to time." Even at the same place and time, the Fourth Amendment's protections might vary if federal officers were not subject to the same statutory constraints as state officers.

We conclude that warrantless arrests for crimes committed in the presence of an arresting officer are reasonable under the Constitution, and that while States are free to regulate such arrests however they desire, state restrictions do not alter the Fourth Amendment's protections.

IV

Moore argues that even if the Constitution allowed his arrest, it did not allow the arresting officers to search him. We have recognized, however, that officers may perform searches incident to constitutionally permissible arrests in order to ensure their safety and safeguard evidence. We have described this rule as covering any "lawful arrest," with constitutional law as the reference point. That is to say, we have equated a lawful arrest with an arrest based on probable cause.

The interests justifying search are present whenever an officer makes an arrest. A search enables officers to safeguard evidence, and, most critically, to ensure their safety during "the extended exposure which follows the taking of a suspect into custody and transporting him to the police station." Officers issuing citations do not face the same danger, and we therefore held in Knowles v. Iowa, (1998), that they do not have the same authority to search. We cannot agree with the Virginia Supreme Court that Knowles controls here. The state officers arrested Moore, and therefore faced the risks that are "an adequate basis for treating all custodial arrests alike for purposes of search justification."

We reaffirm against a novel challenge what we have signaled for more than half a century. When officers have probable cause to believe that a person has committed a crime in their presence, the Fourth Amendment permits them to make an arrest, and to search the suspect in order to safeguard evidence and ensure their own safety. The judgment of the Supreme Court of Virginia is reversed, and the case is remanded for further proceedings not inconsistent with this opinion.

Chapter 3

THE EXCLUSIONARY RULE

D. Exceptions to the Exclusionary Rule (casebook page 317)

In *Herring v. United States*, the Supreme Court created a major new exception to the exclusionary rule: it applies only to police action that is deliberate or reckless or grossly negligent, or the result of systemic department violations.

Herring v. United States
129 S.Ct. 695 (2009)

Chief Justice ROBERTS delivered the opinion of the Court.

The Fourth Amendment forbids "unreasonable searches and seizures," and this usually requires the police to have probable cause or a warrant before making an arrest. What if an officer reasonably believes there is an outstanding arrest warrant, but that belief turns out to be wrong because of a negligent bookkeeping error by another police employee? The parties here agree that the ensuing arrest is still a violation of the Fourth Amendment, but dispute whether contraband found during a search incident to that arrest must be excluded in a later prosecution.

Our cases establish that such suppression is not an automatic consequence of a Fourth Amendment violation. Instead, the question turns on the culpability of the police and the potential of exclusion to deter wrongful police conduct. Here the error was the result of isolated negligence attenuated from the arrest. We hold that in these circumstances the jury should not be barred from considering all the evidence.

I

On July 7, 2004, Investigator Mark Anderson learned that Bennie Dean Herring had driven to the Coffee County Sheriff's Department to retrieve something from his impounded truck. Herring was no stranger to law enforcement, and Anderson asked the county's warrant clerk, Sandy Pope, to check for any outstanding warrants for Herring's arrest. When she found none, Anderson asked Pope to check with Sharon Morgan, her counterpart in neighboring Dale County. After checking Dale County's computer database, Morgan replied that there was an active arrest warrant for Herring's failure to appear on a felony charge. Pope relayed the information to Anderson and asked Morgan to fax over a copy of the warrant as confirmation. Anderson and a deputy followed Herring as he left the impound lot, pulled him over, and arrested him. A search incident to the arrest revealed methamphetamine in Herring's pocket, and a pistol (which as a felon he could not possess) in his vehicle.

There had, however, been a mistake about the warrant. The Dale County sheriff's computer records are supposed to correspond to actual arrest warrants, which the office also maintains. But when Morgan went to the files to retrieve the actual warrant to fax to Pope, Morgan was unable to find it. She called a court clerk and learned that the warrant had been recalled five months earlier. Normally when a warrant is recalled the court clerk's office or a judge's chambers calls Morgan, who enters the information in the sheriff's computer database and disposes of the physical copy. For whatever reason, the information about the recall of the warrant for Herring did not appear in the database. Morgan immediately called Pope to alert her to the mixup, and Pope contacted Anderson over a secure radio. This all unfolded in 10 to 15 minutes, but Herring had already been arrested and found with the gun and drugs, just a few hundred yards from the sheriff's office.

Herring was indicted in the District Court for the Middle District of Alabama for illegally possessing the gun and drugs, violations of 18 U.S.C. §922(g)(1) and 21 U.S.C. §844(a). He moved to suppress the evidence on the ground that his initial arrest had been illegal because the warrant had been rescinded.

II

When a probable-cause determination was based on reasonable but mistaken assumptions, the person subjected to a search or seizure has not necessarily been the victim of a constitutional violation. The very phrase "probable cause" confirms that the Fourth Amendment does not demand all possible precision. And whether the error can be traced to a mistake by a state actor or some other source may bear on the analysis. For purposes of deciding this case, however, we accept the parties' assumption that there was a Fourth Amendment violation. The issue is whether the exclusionary rule should be applied.

A

The Fourth Amendment protects "[t]he right of the people to be secure in their persons, houses, papers, and effects, against unreasonable searches and seizures," but "contains no provision expressly precluding the use of evidence obtained in violation of its commands," *Arizona v. Evans* (1995). Nonetheless, our decisions establish an exclusionary rule that, when applicable, forbids the use of improperly obtained evidence at trial. We have stated that this judicially created rule is "designed to safeguard Fourth Amendment rights generally through its deterrent effect."

In analyzing the applicability of the rule, we must consider the actions of all the police officers involved. The Coffee County officers did nothing improper.

Indeed, the error was noticed so quickly because Coffee County requested a faxed confirmation of the warrant.

The Eleventh Circuit concluded, however, that somebody in Dale County should have updated the computer database to reflect the recall of the arrest warrant. The court also concluded that this error was negligent, but did not find it to be reckless or deliberate. That fact is crucial to our holding that this error is not enough by itself to require "the extreme sanction of exclusion."

B

1. The fact that a Fourth Amendment violation occurred—*i.e.*, that a search or arrest was unreasonable—does not necessarily mean that the exclusionary rule applies. Indeed, exclusion "has always been our last resort, not our first impulse," *Hudson v. Michigan*, (2006), and our precedents establish important principles that constrain application of the exclusionary rule.

   First, the exclusionary rule is not an individual right and applies only where it " 'result[s] in appreciable deterrence.' " We have repeatedly rejected the argument that exclusion is a necessary consequence of a Fourth Amendment violation. Instead we have focused on the efficacy of the rule in deterring Fourth Amendment violations in the future.

   In addition, the benefits of deterrence must outweigh the costs. "We have never suggested that the exclusionary rule must apply in every circumstance in which it might provide marginal deterrence." "[T]o the extent that application of the exclusionary rule could provide some incremental deterrent, that possible benefit must be weighed against [its] substantial social costs." The principal cost of applying the rule is, of course, letting guilty and possibly dangerous defendants go free—something that "offends basic concepts of the criminal justice system." "[T]he rule's costly toll upon truth-seeking and law enforcement objectives presents a high obstacle for those urging [its] application."

   These principles are reflected in the holding of *Leon*: When police act under a warrant that is invalid for lack of probable cause, the exclusionary rule does not apply if the police acted "in objectively reasonable reliance" on the subsequently invalidated search warrant. We (perhaps confusingly) called this objectively reasonable reliance "good faith."

   Shortly thereafter we extended these holdings to warrantless administrative searches performed in good-faith reliance on a statute later declared unconstitutional. Finally, we applied this good-faith rule to police who reasonably relied on mistaken information in a court's database that an arrest warrant was outstanding. We held that a mistake made by a judicial employee could not give rise to exclusion for three reasons: The exclusionary rule was crafted to curb police rather than judicial misconduct; court employees were unlikely to try to subvert the Fourth Amendment; and "most important, there [was] no basis for believing that application of the exclusionary rule in [those] circumstances" would have any significant effect in deterring the errors. [*Arizona v.*] *Evans* left unresolved "whether the evidence should be suppressed if police personnel were responsible for the error," an issue not argued by the State in that case, but one that we now confront.

2. Anticipating the good-faith exception to the exclusionary rule, Judge Friendly wrote that "[t]he beneficent aim of the exclusionary rule to deter police misconduct can be sufficiently accomplished by a practice . . . outlawing evidence obtained by flagrant or deliberate violation of rights." The Bill of Rights as a Code of Criminal Procedure, 53 Calif. L.Rev. 929, 953 (1965). Indeed, the abuses that gave rise to the exclusionary rule featured intentional conduct that was patently unconstitutional.

3. To trigger the exclusionary rule, police conduct must be sufficiently deliberate that exclusion can meaningfully deter it, and sufficiently culpable that such deterrence is worth the price paid by the justice system. As laid out in our cases, the exclusionary rule serves to deter deliberate, reckless, or grossly negligent conduct, or in some circumstances recurring or systemic negligence. The error in this case does not rise to that level.[1]

Our decision in *Franks v. Delaware* (1978), provides an analogy. In *Franks*, we held that police negligence in obtaining a warrant did not even rise to the level of a Fourth Amendment violation, let alone meet the more stringent test for triggering the exclusionary rule. We held that the Constitution allowed defendants, in some circumstances, "to challenge the truthfulness of factual statements made in an affidavit supporting the warrant," even after the warrant had issued. If those false statements were necessary to the Magistrate Judge's probable-cause determination, the warrant would be "voided." But we did not find all false statements relevant: "There must be allegations of deliberate falsehood or of reckless disregard for the truth," and "[a]llegations of negligence or innocent mistake are insufficient."

Both this case and *Franks* concern false information provided by police. Under *Franks*, negligent police miscommunications in the course of acquiring a warrant do not provide a basis to rescind a warrant and render a search or arrest invalid. Here, the miscommunications occurred in a different context—after the warrant had been issued and recalled—but that fact should not require excluding the evidence obtained.

The pertinent analysis of deterrence and culpability is objective, not an "inquiry into the subjective awareness of arresting officers." We have already held that "our good-faith inquiry is confined to the objectively ascertainable question whether a reasonably well trained officer would have known that

---

1. We do not quarrel with Justice Ginsburg's claim that "liability for negligence . . . creates an incentive to act with greater care," and we do not suggest that the exclusion of this evidence could have *no* deterrent effect. But our cases require any deterrence to "be weighed against the 'substantial social costs exacted by the exclusionary rule,' " and here exclusion is not worth the cost. [Footnote by the Court]

the search was illegal" in light of "all of the circumstances." These circumstances frequently include a particular officer's knowledge and experience, but that does not make the test any more subjective than the one for probable cause, which looks to an officer's knowledge and experience, but not his subjective intent.

4. We do not suggest that all recordkeeping errors by the police are immune from the exclusionary rule. In this case, however, the conduct at issue was not so objectively culpable as to require exclusion. In *Leon* we held that "the marginal or nonexistent benefits produced by suppressing evidence obtained in objectively reasonable reliance on a subsequently invalidated search warrant cannot justify the substantial costs of exclusion." The same is true when evidence is obtained in objectively reasonable reliance on a subsequently recalled warrant.

If the police have been shown to be reckless in maintaining a warrant system, or to have knowingly made false entries to lay the groundwork for future false arrests, exclusion would certainly be justified under our cases should such misconduct cause a Fourth Amendment violation. Petitioner's fears that our decision will cause police departments to deliberately keep their officers ignorant are thus unfounded. The dissent also adverts to the possible unreliability of a number of databases not relevant to this case. In a case where systemic errors were demonstrated, it might be reckless for officers to rely on an unreliable warrant system. But there is no evidence that errors in Dale County's system are routine or widespread.

* * *

Petitioner's claim that police negligence automatically triggers suppression cannot be squared with the principles underlying the exclusionary rule, as they have been explained in our cases. In light of our repeated holdings that the deterrent effect of suppression must be substantial and outweigh any harm to the justice system, we conclude that when police mistakes are the result of negligence such as that described here, rather than systemic error or reckless disregard of constitutional requirements, any marginal deterrence does not "pay its way." In such a case, the criminal should not "go free because the constable has blundered." *People v. Defore*, (1926) (opinion of the Court by CARDOZO, J.).

Justice GINSBURG, with whom Justice STEVENS, Justice SOUTER, and Justice BREYER join, dissenting.

Petitioner Bennie Dean Herring was arrested, and subjected to a search incident to his arrest, although no warrant was outstanding against him, and the police lacked probable cause to believe he was engaged in criminal activity. The arrest and ensuing search therefore violated Herring's Fourth Amendment right "to be secure . . . against unreasonable searches and seizures." The Court of Appeals so determined, and the Government does not contend otherwise.

The exclusionary rule provides redress for Fourth Amendment violations by placing the government in the position it would have been in had there been no unconstitutional arrest and search. The rule thus strongly encourages police compliance with the Fourth Amendment in the future. The Court, however, holds the rule inapplicable because careless recordkeeping by the police—not flagrant or deliberate misconduct—accounts for Herring's arrest.

I would not so constrict the domain of the exclusionary rule and would hold the rule dispositive of this case: "[I]f courts are to have any power to discourage [police] error of [the kind here at issue], it must be through the application of the exclusionary rule." The unlawful search in this case was contested in court because the police found methamphetamine in Herring's pocket and a pistol in his truck. But the "most serious impact" of the Court's holding will be on innocent persons "wrongfully arrested based on erroneous information [carelessly maintained] in a computer data base."

[I]

A

The Court states that the exclusionary rule is not a defendant's right, rather, it is simply a remedy applicable only when suppression would result in appreciable deterrence that outweighs the cost to the justice system. The Court's discussion invokes a view of the exclusionary rule famously held by renowned jurists Henry J. Friendly and Benjamin Nathan Cardozo. Over 80 years ago, Cardozo, then seated on the New York Court of Appeals, commented critically on the federal exclusionary rule, which had not yet been applied to the States. He suggested that in at least some cases the rule exacted too high a price from the criminal justice system. See *People v. Defore*, (1926). In words often quoted, Cardozo questioned whether the criminal should "go free because the constable has blundered." Judge Friendly later elaborated on Cardozo's query. "The sole reason for exclusion," Friendly wrote, "is that experience has demonstrated this to be the only effective method for deterring the police from violating the Constitution." He thought it excessive, in light of the rule's aim to deter police conduct, to require exclusion when the constable had merely "blundered"—when a police officer committed a technical error in an on-the-spot judgment, or made a "slight and unintentional miscalculation."

B

Others have described "a more majestic conception" of the Fourth Amendment and its adjunct, the exclusionary rule. Protective of the fundamental "right of the people to be secure in their persons, houses, papers, and effects," the Amendment "is a constraint on the power of the sovereign, not merely on some of its agents." I share that vision of the Amendment.

The exclusionary rule is "a remedy necessary to ensure that" the Fourth Amendment's prohibitions "are observed in fact." The rule's service as an essential auxiliary to the Amendment earlier inclined the Court to hold the two inseparable.

Beyond doubt, a main objective of the rule "is to deter—to compel respect for the constitutional guaranty in the only effectively available way—by removing the incentive to disregard it." But the rule also serves other important purposes: It "enabl[es] the judiciary to avoid the taint of partnership in official lawlessness," and it "assur[es] the people—all potential victims of unlawful government conduct—that the government would not profit from its lawless behavior, thus minimizing the risk of seriously undermining popular trust in government."

The exclusionary rule, it bears emphasis, is often the only remedy effective to redress a Fourth Amendment violation. Civil liability will not lie for "the vast majority of [F]ourth [A]mendment violations—the frequent infringements motivated by commendable zeal, not condemnable malice." Criminal prosecutions or administrative sanctions against the offending officers and injunctive relief against widespread violations are an even farther cry.

[II]

The Court maintains that Herring's case is one in which the exclusionary rule could have scant deterrent effect and therefore would not "pay its way." I disagree.

A

The exclusionary rule, the Court suggests, is capable of only marginal deterrence when the misconduct at issue is merely careless, not intentional or reckless. The suggestion runs counter to a foundational premise of tort law—that liability for negligence, *i.e.*, lack of due care, creates an incentive to act with greater care.

That the mistake here involved the failure to make a computer entry hardly means that application of the exclusionary rule would have minimal value. "Just as the risk of *respondeat superior* liability encourages employers to supervise . . . their employees' conduct [more carefully], so the risk of exclusion of evidence encourages policymakers and systems managers to monitor the performance of the systems they install and the personnel employed to operate those systems."

Consider the potential impact of a decision applying the exclusionary rule in this case. As earlier observed, the record indicates that there is no electronic connection between the warrant database of the Dale County Sheriff's Department and that of the County Circuit Clerk's office, which is located in the basement of the same building. When a warrant is recalled, one of the "many different people that have access to th[e] warrants," must find the hard copy of the warrant in the "two or three different places" where the department houses warrants, return it to the Clerk's office, and manually update the Department's database. The record reflects no routine practice of checking the database for accuracy, and the failure to remove the entry for Herring's warrant was not discovered until Investigator Anderson sought to pursue Herring five months later. Is it not altogether obvious that the Department could take further precautions to ensure the integrity of its database? The Sheriff's Department "is in a position to remedy the situation and might well do so if the exclusionary rule is there to remove the incentive to do otherwise."

B

Is the potential deterrence here worth the costs it imposes? In light of the paramount importance of accurate recordkeeping in law enforcement, I would answer yes, and next explain why, as I see it, Herring's motion presents a particularly strong case for suppression.

Electronic databases form the nervous system of contemporary criminal justice operations. In recent years, their breadth and influence have dramatically expanded. Police today can access databases that include not only the updated National Crime Information Center (NCIC), but also terrorist watchlists, the Federal Government's employee eligibility system, and various commercial databases. Moreover, States are actively expanding information sharing between jurisdictions. As a result, law enforcement has an increasing supply of information within its easy electronic reach.

The risk of error stemming from these databases is not slim. Herring's *amici* warn that law enforcement databases are insufficiently monitored and often out of date. Government reports describe, for example, flaws in NCIC databases, terrorist watchlist databases, and databases associated with the Federal Government's employment eligibility verification system.

Inaccuracies in expansive, interconnected collections of electronic information raise grave concerns for individual liberty. "The offense to the dignity of the citizen who is arrested, handcuffed, and searched on a public street simply because some bureaucrat has failed to maintain an accurate computer data base" is evocative of the use of general warrants that so outraged the authors of our Bill of Rights.

C

The Court assures that "exclusion would certainly be justified" if "the police have been shown to be reckless in maintaining a warrant system, or to have knowingly made false entries to lay the groundwork for future false arrests." This concession provides little comfort.

First, by restricting suppression to bookkeeping errors that are deliberate or reckless, the majority leaves Herring, and others like him, with no remedy for violations of their constitutional rights.

Second, I doubt that police forces already possess sufficient incentives to maintain up-to-date records. The Government argues that police have no desire to send officers out on arrests unnecessarily, because arrests consume resources and place officers in danger. The facts of this case do not fit that description of police motivation. Here the officer wanted to arrest Herring and consulted the Department's records to legitimate his predisposition.

Third, even when deliberate or reckless conduct is afoot, the Court's assurance will often be an empty promise: How is an impecunious defendant to make the required showing? If the answer is that a defendant is entitled to discovery (and if necessary, an audit of police databases), then the Court has imposed a considerable administrative burden on courts and law enforcement.[2]

[IV]

Negligent recordkeeping errors by law enforcement threaten individual liberty, are susceptible to deterrence by the exclusionary rule, and cannot be remedied effectively through other means. Such errors present no occasion to further erode the exclusionary rule. The rule "is needed to make the Fourth Amendment something real; a guarantee that does not carry with it the exclusion of evidence obtained by its violation is a chimera." In keeping with the rule's "core concerns," suppression should have attended the unconstitutional search in this case.

Justice BREYER, with whom Justice SOUTER joins, dissenting.

I agree with Justice GINSBURG and join her dissent. I write separately to note one additional supporting factor that I believe important. In *Arizona v. Evans* (1995), we held that recordkeeping errors made by a court clerk do not trigger the exclusionary rule, so long as the police reasonably relied upon the court clerk's recordkeeping. The rationale for our decision was premised on a distinction between judicial errors and police errors, and we gave several reasons for recognizing that distinction.

First, we noted that "the exclusionary rule was historically designed as a means of deterring *police* misconduct, not mistakes by court employees." *Second*, we found "no evidence that court employees are inclined to ignore or subvert the Fourth Amendment or that lawlessness among these actors requires application of the extreme sanction of exclusion." *Third*, we recognized that there was "no basis for believing that application of the exclusionary rule . . . [would] have a significant effect on court employees responsible for informing the police that a warrant has been quashed. Because court clerks are not adjuncts to the law enforcement team engaged in the often competitive enterprise of ferreting out crime, they have no stake in the outcome of particular criminal prosecutions." Taken together, these reasons explain why police recordkeeping errors should be treated differently than judicial ones.

Other cases applying the "good faith" exception to the exclusionary rule have similarly recognized the distinction between police errors and errors made by others, such as judicial officers or legislatures.

Distinguishing between police recordkeeping errors and judicial ones not only is consistent with our precedent, but also is far easier for courts to administer

---

2. It is not clear how the Court squares its focus on deliberate conduct with its recognition that application of the exclusionary rule does not require inquiry into the mental state of the police. [Footnote by Justice GINSBURG]

than THE CHIEF JUSTICE's case-by-case, multifactored inquiry into the degree of police culpability. I therefore would apply the exclusionary rule when police personnel are responsible for a recordkeeping error that results in a Fourth Amendment violation.

The need for a clear line, and the recognition of such a line in our precedent, are further reasons in support of the outcome that Justice GINSBURG's dissent would reach.

Chapter 4

POLICE INTERROGATION AND THE PRIVILEGE AGAINST SELF-INCRIMINATION

C. The Sixth Amendment Right to Counsel and Police Interrogations

3. Waivers (casebook page 481)

In *Jackson v. Michigan* (casebook p. 481), the Supreme Court held that once counsel had been appointed under the Sixth Amendment there could not be questioning without the presence of the police. In *Montejo v. Louisiana*, the Court overruled *Jackson v. Michigan.* The Court stressed, though, that if the right to counsel is involved under the Fifth Amendment, *Edwards v. Arizona* still precludes police from eliciting incriminating statements without the presence of counsel.

Montejo v. Louisiana
129 S.Ct. 2079 (2009)

Justice SCALIA delivered the opinion of the Court.

We consider in this case the scope and continued viability of the rule announced by this Court in *Michigan v. Jackson* (1986), forbidding police to initiate interrogation of a criminal defendant once he has requested counsel at an arraignment or similar proceeding.

I

Petitioner Jesse Montejo was arrested on September 6, 2002, in connection with the robbery and murder of Lewis Ferrari, who had been found dead in his own home one day earlier. Suspicion quickly focused on Jerry Moore, a disgruntled former employee of Ferrari's dry cleaning business. Police sought to question Montejo, who was a known associate of Moore.

Montejo waived his rights under *Miranda v. Arizona* (1966), and was interrogated at the sheriff's office by police detectives through the late afternoon and evening of September 6 and the early morning of September 7. During the interrogation, Montejo repeatedly changed his account of the crime, at first claiming that he had only driven Moore to the victim's home, and ultimately admitting that he had shot and killed Ferrari in the course of a botched burglary. These police interrogations were videotaped.

On September 10, Montejo was brought before a judge for what is known in Louisiana as a "72-hour hearing"—a preliminary hearing required under state law. Although the proceedings were not transcribed, the minute record indicates what transpired: "The defendant being charged with First Degree Murder, Court ordered N[o] Bond set in this matter. Further, Court ordered the Office of Indigent Defender be appointed to represent the defendant."

Later that same day, two police detectives visited Montejo back at the prison and requested that he accompany them on an excursion to locate the murder weapon (which Montejo had earlier indicated he had thrown into a lake). After some back-and-forth, the substance of which remains in dispute, Montejo was again read his *Miranda* rights and agreed to go along; during the excursion, he wrote an inculpatory letter of apology to the victim's widow. Only upon their return did Montejo finally meet his court-appointed attorney, who was quite upset that the detectives had interrogated his client in his absence.

At trial, the letter of apology was admitted over defense objection. The jury convicted Montejo of first-degree murder, and he was sentenced to death.

The Louisiana Supreme Court affirmed the conviction and sentence. As relevant here, the court rejected Montejo's argument that under the rule of *Jackson*, the letter should have been suppressed. *Jackson* held that "if police initiate interrogation after a defendant's assertion, at an arraignment or similar proceeding, of his right to counsel, any waiver of the defendant's right to counsel for that police-initiated interrogation is invalid."

II

[II]

Montejo's solution is untenable as a theoretical and doctrinal matter. Under his approach, once a defendant is *represented* by counsel, police may not initiate any further interrogation. Such a rule would be entirely untethered from the original rationale of *Jackson*.

A

It is worth emphasizing first what is *not* in dispute or at stake here. Under our precedents, once the adversary judicial process has been initiated, the Sixth Amendment guarantees a defendant the right to have counsel present at all "critical" stages of the criminal proceedings. Interrogation by the State is such a stage.

Our precedents also place beyond doubt that the Sixth Amendment right to counsel may be waived by a defendant, so long as relinquishment of the right is voluntary, knowing, and intelligent. The defendant may waive the right whether or not he is already represented by counsel; the decision to waive need not itself be counseled. And when a defendant is read his *Miranda* rights (which include the right to have counsel present during interrogation) and agrees to waive those rights, that typically does the trick, even though the *Miranda* rights purportedly have their source in the *Fifth* Amendment.

The *only* question raised by this case, and the only one addressed by the *Jackson* rule, is whether courts must *presume* that such a waiver is invalid under certain circumstances. We created such a presumption in *Jackson* by analogy to a similar prophylactic rule established to protect the Fifth Amendment based *Miranda* right to have counsel present at any custodial interrogation. *Edwards v. Arizona* (1981), decided that once "an accused has invoked his right to have counsel present during custodial interrogation . . . [he] is not subject to further interrogation by the authorities until counsel has been made available," unless he initiates the contact.

The *Edwards* rule is "designed to prevent police from badgering a defendant into waiving his previously asserted *Miranda* rights." It does this by presuming his postassertion statements to be involuntary, "even where the suspect executes a waiver and his statements would be considered voluntary under traditional standards." This prophylactic rule thus "protect[s] a suspect's voluntary choice not to speak outside his lawyer's presence."

Jackson represented a "wholesale importation of the *Edwards* rule into the Sixth Amendment." The *Jackson* Court decided that a request for counsel at an arraignment should be treated as an invocation of the Sixth Amendment right to counsel "at every critical stage of the prosecution," despite doubt that defendants "actually inten[d] their request for counsel to encompass representation during any further questioning," because doubts must be "resolved in favor of protecting the constitutional claim." Citing *Edwards*, the Court held that any subsequent waiver would thus be "insufficient to justify police-initiated interrogation." In other words, we presume such waivers involuntary "based on the supposition that suspects who assert their right to counsel are unlikely to waive that right voluntarily" in subsequent interactions with police.

The dissent presents us with a revisionist view of *Jackson*. The defendants' *request* for counsel, it contends, was important only because it proved that counsel *had been appointed*. Such a non sequitur (nowhere alluded to in the case) hardly needs rebuttal. Proceeding from this fanciful premise, the dissent claims that the decision actually established "a rule designed to safeguard a defendant's right to rely on the assistance of counsel," not one "designed to prevent police badgering." To safeguard the right to assistance of counsel from *what*? From a knowing and voluntary waiver by the defendant himself? Unless the dissent seeks to prevent a defendant altogether from waiving his Sixth Amendment rights, *i.e.*, to "imprison a man in his privileges and call it the Constitution,"—a view with zero support in reason, history or case law—the answer must be: from police pressure, *i.e.*, badgering. The antibadgering rationale is the only way to make sense of *Jackson*'s repeated citations of *Edwards*, and the only way to reconcile the opinion with our waiver jurisprudence.

B

With this understanding of what *Jackson* stands for and whence it came, it should be clear that Montejo's interpretation of that decision—that no *represented* defendant can ever be approached by the State and asked to consent to interrogation—is off the mark. When a court appoints counsel for an indigent defendant in the absence of any request on his part, there is no basis for a presumption that any subsequent waiver of the right to counsel will be involuntary. There is no "*initial* election" to exercise the right, that must be preserved through a prophylactic rule against later waivers. No reason exists to assume that a defendant like Montejo, who has done *nothing at all* to express his intentions with respect to his Sixth Amendment rights, would not be perfectly amenable to speaking with the police without having counsel present. And no reason exists to prohibit the police from inquiring. *Edwards* and *Jackson* are meant to prevent police from badgering defendants into changing their minds about their rights, but a defendant who never asked for counsel has not yet made up his mind in the first instance.

The dissent's argument to the contrary rests on a flawed *a fortiori*: "If a defendant is entitled to protection from police-initiated interrogation under the Sixth Amendment when he merely *requests* a lawyer, he is even more obviously entitled to such protection when he has *secured* a lawyer." The question in *Jackson*, however, was not whether respondents were entitled to counsel (they unquestionably were), but "whether respondents validly waived their right to counsel," and even if it is reasonable to presume from a defendant's *request* for counsel that any subsequent waiver of the right was coerced, no such presumption can seriously be entertained when a lawyer was merely "secured" on the defendant's behalf, by the State itself, as a matter of course. Of course, reading the dissent's analysis, one would have no idea that Montejo executed any waiver at all.

In practice, Montejo's rule would prevent police-initiated interrogation entirely once the Sixth Amendment right attaches, at least in those States that appoint counsel promptly without request from the defendant. As the dissent in *Jackson* pointed out, with no expressed disagreement from the majority, the opinion "most assuredly [did] *not* hold that the *Edwards per se* rule prohibiting all police-initiated interrogations applies from the moment the defendant's Sixth Amendment right to counsel attaches, with or without a request for counsel by the defendant." That would have constituted a "shockingly dramatic restructuring of the balance this Court has traditionally struck between the rights of the defendant and those of the larger society."

Montejo's rule appears to have its theoretical roots in codes of legal ethics, not the Sixth Amendment. The American Bar Association's Model Rules of Professional Conduct (which nearly all States have adopted into law in whole or in part) mandate that "a lawyer shall not communicate about the subject of [a] representation with a party the lawyer knows to be represented by another lawyer in the matter, unless the lawyer has the consent of the other lawyer or is authorized to do so by law or a court order." Model Rule 4.2 (2008). But the Constitution does not codify the ABA's Model Rules, and does not make investigating police officers lawyers. Montejo's proposed rule is both broader and narrower than the Model Rule. Broader, because Montejo would apply it to all agents of the State, including the detectives who interrogated him, while the ethical rule governs only lawyers. And narrower, because he agrees that if a defendant initiates contact with the police, they may talk freely—whereas a lawyer could be sanctioned for interviewing a represented party even if that party "initiates" the communication and consents to the interview.

The upshot is that even on *Jackson*'s own terms, it would be completely unjustified to presume that a defendant's consent to police-initiated interrogation was involuntary or coerced simply because he had previously been appointed a lawyer.

[III]

We do not think that *stare decisis* requires us to expand significantly the holding of a prior decision—fundamentally revising its theoretical basis in the process—in order to cure its practical deficiencies. To the contrary, the fact that a decision has proved "unworkable" is a traditional ground for overruling it. Accordingly, we called for supplemental briefing addressed to the question whether *Michigan v. Jackson* should be overruled.

Beyond workability, the relevant factors in deciding whether to adhere to the principle of *stare decisis* include the antiquity of the precedent, the reliance interests at stake, and of course whether the decision was well reasoned. The first two cut in favor of abandoning *Jackson*: the opinion is only two decades old, and eliminating it would not upset expectations. Any criminal defendant learned enough to order his affairs based on the rule announced in *Jackson* would also be perfectly capable of interacting with the police on his own. Of course it is likely true that police and prosecutors have been trained to comply with *Jackson*, but that is hardly a basis for retaining it as a constitutional requirement. If a State *wishes* to abstain from requesting interviews with represented defendants when counsel is not present, it obviously may continue to do so.

Which brings us to the strength of *Jackson*'s reasoning. When this Court creates a prophylactic rule in order to protect a constitutional right, the relevant "reasoning" is the weighing of the rule's benefits against its costs. "The value of any prophylactic rule . . . must be assessed not only on the basis of what is gained, but also on the basis of what is lost." We think that the marginal benefits of *Jackson* (viz., the number of confessions obtained coercively that are suppressed by its bright-line rule and would otherwise have been admitted) are dwarfed by its substantial costs (viz., hindering "society's compelling interest in finding, convicting, and punishing those who violate the law.")

What does the *Jackson* rule actually achieve by way of preventing unconstitutional conduct? Recall that the purpose of the rule is to preclude the State from badgering defendants into waiving their previously asserted rights. The effect of this badgering might be to coerce a waiver, which would render the subsequent interrogation a violation of the Sixth Amendment. Even though involuntary waivers are invalid even apart from mistakes are of course possible when courts conduct case-by-case voluntariness review. A bright-line rule like that adopted in *Jackson* ensures that no fruits of interrogations made possible by badgering-induced involuntary waivers are ever erroneously admitted at trial.

But without *Jackson*, how many would be? The answer is few if any. The principal reason is that the Court has already taken substantial other, overlapping measures toward the same end. Under *Miranda's* prophylactic protection of the right against compelled self-incrimination, any suspect subject to custodial interrogation has the right to have a lawyer present if he so requests, and to be advised of that right. Under *Edwards'* prophylactic protection of the *Miranda* right, once such a defendant "has invoked his right to have counsel present," interrogation must stop. And under *Minnick's* prophylactic protection of the *Edwards* right, no subsequent interrogation may take place until counsel is present, "whether or not the accused has consulted with his attorney."

These three layers of prophylaxis are sufficient. Under the *Miranda-Edwards-Minnick* line of cases (which is not in doubt), a defendant who does not want to speak to the police without counsel present need only say as much when he is first approached and given the *Miranda* warnings. At that point, not only must the immediate contact end, but "badgering" by later requests is prohibited. If that regime suffices to protect the integrity of "a suspect's voluntary choice not to speak outside his lawyer's presence" before his arraignment, it is hard to see why it would not also suffice to protect that same choice after arraignment, when Sixth Amendment rights have attached. And if so, then *Jackson* is simply superfluous.

It is true, as Montejo points out in his supplemental brief, that the doctrine established by *Miranda* and *Edwards* is designed to protect Fifth Amendment, not Sixth Amendment, rights. But that is irrelevant. What matters is that these cases, like *Jackson*, protect the right to have counsel during custodial interrogation — which right happens to be guaranteed (once the adversary judicial process has begun) by *two* sources of law. Since the right under both sources is waived using the same procedure, doctrines ensuring voluntariness of the Fifth Amendment waiver simultaneously ensure the voluntariness of the Sixth Amendment waiver.

Montejo also correctly observes that the *Miranda-Edwards* regime is narrower than *Jackson* in one respect: The former applies only in the context of custodial interrogation. If the defendant is not in custody then those decisions do not apply; nor do they govern other, noninterrogative types of interactions between the defendant and the State (like pretrial lineups). However, those uncovered situations are the *least* likely to pose a risk of coerced waivers. When a defendant is not in custody, he is in control, and need only shut his door or walk away to avoid police badgering. And noninterrogative interactions with the State do not involve the "inherently compelling pressures," that one might reasonably fear could lead to involuntary waivers.

Jackson was policy driven, and if that policy is being adequately served through other means, there is no reason to retain its rule. *Miranda* and the cases that elaborate upon it already guarantee not simply noncoercion in the traditional sense, but what Justice *Harlan* referred to as "voluntariness with a vengeance." There is no need to take *Jackson's* further step of requiring voluntariness on stilts.

On the other side of the equation are the costs of adding the bright-line *Jackson* rule on top of *Edwards* and other extant protections. The principal cost of applying any exclusionary rule "is, of course, letting guilty and possibly dangerous criminals go free . . . ." *Jackson* not only "operates to invalidate a confession given by the free choice of suspects who have received proper advice of their *Miranda* rights but waived them nonetheless," but also deters law enforcement officers from even trying to obtain voluntary confessions. The "ready ability to obtain uncoerced confessions is not an evil but an unmitigated good." Without these confessions, crimes go unsolved and criminals unpunished. These are not negligible costs, and in our view the *Jackson* Court gave them too short shrift.

In sum, when the marginal benefits of the *Jackson* rule are weighed against its substantial costs to the truth-seeking process and the criminal justice system, we readily conclude that the rule does not "pay its way." *Michigan v. Jackson* should be and now is overruled.

Justice STEVENS, with whom Justice SOUTER and Justice GINSBURG join, and with whom Justice BREYER joins.

Today the Court properly concludes that the Louisiana Supreme Court's parsimonious reading of our decision in *Michigan v. Jackson* (1986), is indefensible. Yet the Court does not reverse. Rather, on its own initiative and without any evidence that the longstanding Sixth Amendment protections established in *Jackson* have caused any harm to the workings of the criminal justice system, the Court rejects *Jackson* outright on the ground that it is "untenable as a theoretical and doctrinal matter." That conclusion rests on a misinterpretation of *Jackson's* rationale and a gross undervaluation of the rule of *stare decisis*. The police interrogation in this case clearly violated petitioner's Sixth Amendment right to counsel.

I

The Sixth Amendment provides that "[i]n all criminal prosecutions, the accused shall enjoy the right . . . to have the Assistance of Counsel for his defence." The right to counsel attaches during "the initiation of adversary judicial criminal proceedings," and it guarantees the assistance of counsel not only during in-court proceedings but during all critical stages, including postarraignment interviews with law enforcement officers.

In *Jackson*, this Court considered whether the Sixth Amendment bars police from interrogating defendants who have requested the appointment of counsel at arraignment. Applying the presumption that such a request constitutes an invocation of the right to counsel "at every critical stage of the prosecution," we held that "a defendant who has been formally charged with a crime and who has requested appointment of counsel at his arraignment" cannot be subject to uncounseled interrogation unless he initiates "exchanges or conversations with the police."

[I]

Today the Court correctly concludes that the Louisiana Supreme Court's holding is "troublesome," "impractical," and "unsound." Instead of reversing the decision of the state court by simply answering the question on which we granted certiorari in a unanimous opinion, however, the majority has decided to change the law. Acting on its own initiative, the majority overrules *Jackson* to correct a "theoretical and doctrinal" problem of its own imagining. A more careful reading of *Jackson* and the Sixth Amendment cases upon which it relied reveals that the rule announced in *Jackson* protects a fundamental right that the Court now dishonors.

The majority's decision to overrule *Jackson* rests on its assumption that *Jackson*'s protective rule was intended to "prevent police from badgering defendants into changing their minds about their rights," just as the rule adopted in *Edwards v. Arizona* (1981), was designed to prevent police from coercing unindicted suspects into revoking their requests for counsel at interrogation. Operating on that limited understanding of the purpose behind *Jackson*'s protective rule, the Court concludes that *Jackson* provides no safeguard not already secured by this Court's Fifth Amendment jurisprudence.

The majority's analysis flagrantly misrepresents *Jackson*'s underlying rationale and the constitutional interests the decision sought to protect. While it is true that the rule adopted in *Jackson* was patterned after the rule in *Edwards*, the *Jackson* opinion does not even mention the anti-badgering considerations that provide the basis for the Court's decision today. Instead, *Jackson* relied primarily on cases discussing the broad protections guaranteed by the Sixth Amendment right to counsel — not its Fifth Amendment counterpart. *Jackson* emphasized that the purpose of the Sixth Amendment is to "protec[t] the unaided layman at critical confrontations with his adversary," by giving him "the right to rely on counsel as a "medium" between him[self] and the State." Underscoring that the commencement of criminal proceedings is a decisive event that transforms a suspect into an accused within the meaning of the Sixth Amendment, we concluded that arraigned defendants are entitled to "at least as much protection" during interrogation as the Fifth Amendment affords unindicted suspects. Thus, although the rules adopted in *Edwards* and *Jackson* are similar, *Jackson* did not rely on the reasoning of *Edwards* but remained firmly rooted in the unique protections afforded to the attorney-client relationship by the Sixth Amendment.

Police Interrogation and the Privilege Against Self-Incrimination

Once *Jackson* is placed in its proper Sixth Amendment context, the majority's justifications for overruling the decision crumble. Ordinarily, this Court is hesitant to disturb past precedent and will do so only when a rule has proven "outdated, ill-founded, unworkable, or otherwise legitimately vulnerable to serious reconsideration." While *stare decisis* is not "an inexorable command," we adhere to it as "the preferred course because it promotes the evenhanded, predictable, and consistent development of legal principles, fosters reliance on judicial decisions, and contributes to the actual and perceived integrity of the judicial process."

Paying lip service to the rule of *stare decisis*, the majority acknowledges that the Court must consider many factors before taking the dramatic step of overruling a past decision. Specifically, the majority focuses on four considerations: the reasoning of the decision, the workability of the rule, the reliance interests at stake, and the antiquity of the precedent. The Court exaggerates the considerations favoring reversal, however, and gives short shrift to the valid considerations favoring retention of the *Jackson* rule.

First, and most central to the Court's decision to overrule *Jackson*, is its assertion that *Jackson*'s " 'reasoning' "—which the Court defines as "the weighing of the [protective] rule's benefits against its costs," does not justify continued application of the rule it created. The balancing test the Court performs, however, depends entirely on its misunderstanding of *Jackson* as a rule designed to prevent police badgering, rather than a rule designed to safeguard a defendant's right to rely on the assistance of counsel.

Next, in order to reach the conclusion that the *Jackson* rule is unworkable, the Court reframes the relevant inquiry, asking not whether the *Jackson* rule as applied for the past quarter century has proved easily administrable, but instead whether the Louisiana Supreme Court's cramped interpretation of that rule is practically workable. The answer to that question, of course, is no. When framed more broadly, however, the evidence is overwhelming that *Jackson*'s simple, bright-line rule has done more to advance effective law enforcement than to undermine it.

In a supplemental brief submitted by lawyers and judges with extensive experience in law enforcement and prosecution, *amici* Larry D. Thompson et al. argue persuasively that *Jackson*'s bright-line rule has provided law enforcement officers with clear guidance, allowed prosecutors to quickly and easily assess whether confessions will be admissible in court, and assisted judges in determining whether a defendant's Sixth Amendment rights have been violated by police interrogation. See generally Thompson. While *amici* acknowledge that "*Jackson* reduces opportunities to interrogate defendants" and "may require exclusion of evidence that could support a criminal conviction," they maintain that "it is a rare case where this rule lets a guilty defendant go free." In short, there is substantial evidence suggesting that *Jackson*'s rule is not only workable, but also desirable from the perspective of law enforcement.

Turning to the reliance interests at stake in the case, the Court rejects the interests of criminal defendants with the flippant observation that any who are knowledgeable enough to rely on *Jackson* are too savvy to need its protections, and casts aside the reliance interests of law enforcement on the ground that police and prosecutors remain free to employ the *Jackson* rule if it suits them. Again as a result of its mistaken understanding of the purpose behind *Jackson*'s protective rule, the Court fails to identify the real reliance interest at issue in this case: the public's interest in knowing that counsel, once secured, may be reasonably relied upon as a medium between the accused and the power of the State. That interest lies at the heart of the Sixth Amendment's guarantee, and is surely worthy of greater consideration than it is given by today's decision.

Finally, although the Court acknowledges that "antiquity" is a factor that counsels in favor of retaining precedent, it concludes that the fact *Jackson* is "only two decades old" cuts "in favor of abandoning" the rule it established. I would have thought that the 23-year existence of a simple bright-line rule would be a factor that cuts in the other direction.

Despite the fact that the rule established in *Jackson* remains relevant, well grounded in constitutional precedent, and easily administrable, the Court today rejects it *sua sponte*. Such a decision can only diminish the public's confidence in the reliability and fairness of our system of justice.

III

Even if *Jackson* had never been decided, it would be clear that Montejo's Sixth Amendment rights were violated. Today's decision eliminates the rule that "any waiver of Sixth Amendment rights given in a discussion initiated by police is presumed invalid" once a defendant has invoked his right to counsel. Nevertheless, under the undisputed facts of this case, there is no sound basis for concluding that Montejo made a knowing and valid waiver of his Sixth Amendment right to counsel before acquiescing in police interrogation following his 72-hour hearing. Because police questioned Montejo without notice to, and outside the presence of, his lawyer, the interrogation violated Montejo's right to counsel even under pre-*Jackson* precedent.

IV

The Court's decision to overrule *Jackson* is unwarranted. Not only does it rest on a flawed doctrinal premise, but the dubious benefits it hopes to achieve are far outweighed by the damage it does to the rule of law and the integrity of the Sixth Amendment right to counsel. Moreover, even apart from the protections afforded by *Jackson*, the police interrogation in this case violated Jesse Montejo's Sixth Amendment right to counsel.

* * *

D. The Sixth Amendment Right to Counsel and Police Interrogation

4. What Is Impermissible Police Eliciting of Statements? (casebook, page 486)

In *Kansas* v. *Ventris*, 129 S.Ct. 1841 (2009), the Court held that statements obtained in violation of the Sixth Amendment right to counsel may be used for impeachment purposes. Donnie Ray Ventris was charged with murder and other crimes. The police placed an informant in his cell with the hope of obtaining incriminating statements, in violation of his Sixth Amendment rights. Ventris made incriminating statements.

At trial, Ventris testified and said that his girlfriend was responsible for the murders. The prosecutor used cellmate as a witness to impeach Ventris' testimony. The Supreme Court held that the statements could be introduced for impeachment purposes even though they were obtained in violation of the Sixth Amendment. Justice Souter, writing for the Court in a 7-2 decision, stated: "Our precedents make clear that the game of excluding tainted evidence for impeachment purposes is not worth the candle. The interests safeguarded by such exclusion are 'outweighed by the need to prevent perjury and to assure the integrity of the trial process.'" The Court said that excluding the statements would add little deterrent effect, but would interfere with the ability of courts to ensure the accuracy of testimony. The Court concluded: "We hold that the informant's testimony, concededly elicited in violation of the Sixth Amendment, was admissible to challenge Ventris's inconsistent testimony at trial."

Chapter 7

BAIL AND PRETRIAL RELEASE

B. Preventative Detention

2. Other Types of Preventative Detention

d. *Enemy Combatants (casebook, page 614)*

On June 12, 2008, the Supreme Court reached its decision in *Boumediene v. Bush*, 128 S.Ct. 2229 (2008) and ruled that the Military Commission Act of 2006 unconstitutionally suspended the right of habeas corpus. For a full discussion of this case, see Chapter 15 (Habeas Corpus).

Chapter 8

DISCOVERY

F.   Final Note (casebook page 646)

In *District Attorney's Office for the Third Judicial Dist. v. Osborne*, 129 S.Ct. _____ (2009), the Supreme Court held that there is no due process right to post-conviction DNA testing. States may enact statutes authorizing such testing, but they are not required to provide such testing in all cases.

Chapter 10

SPEEDY TRIAL RIGHTS

C. Due Process and Speedy Trial Rights

2. Post-Charging Delay and Speedy Trial Rights

b. *Constitutional Protections (casebook page 695)*

If appointed defense counsel delays, does this delay weigh as a factor against a defendant who seeks dismissal of the case on Speedy Trial grounds? The Supreme Court decided that issue in *Vermont v. Brillon.*

Vermont v. Brillon
129 S. Ct. 1283 (2009)

Justice GINSBURG delivered the opinion of the Court.

This case concerns the *Sixth Amendment* guarantee that "[i]n all criminal prosecutions, the accused shall enjoy the right to a speedy . . . trial." Michael Brillon, defendant below, respondent here, was arrested in July 2001 on felony domestic assault and habitual offender charges. Nearly three years later, in June 2004, he was tried by jury, found guilty as charged, and sentenced to 12 to 20 years in prison. The Vermont Supreme Court vacated Brillon's conviction and held that the charges against him must be dismissed because he had been denied his right to a speedy trial.

During the time between Brillon's arrest and his trial, at least six different attorneys were appointed to represent him. Brillon "fired" the first, who served from July 2001 to February 2002. His third lawyer, who served from March 2002 until June 2002, was allowed to withdraw when he reported that Brillon had threatened his life. The Vermont Supreme Court charged against Brillon the delays associated with those periods, but charged against the State periods in which assigned counsel failed "to move the case forward."

We hold that the Vermont Supreme Court erred in ranking assigned counsel essentially as state actors in the criminal justice system. Assigned counsel, just as retained counsel, act on behalf of their clients, and delays sought by counsel are ordinarily attributable to the defendants they represent. For a total of some six months of the time that elapsed between Brillon's arrest and his trial, Brillon lacked an attorney. The State may be charged with those months if the gaps resulted from the trial court's failure to appoint replacement counsel with dispatch.

Similarly, the State may bear responsibility if there is "a breakdown in the public defender system." But, as the Vermont Supreme Court acknowledged, the record does not establish any such institutional breakdown.

I

On July 27, 2001, Michael Brillon was arrested after striking his girlfriend. Three days later he was arraigned in state court in Bennington County, Vermont and charged with felony domestic assault. His alleged status as a habitual offender exposed him to a potential life sentence. The court ordered him held without bail.

Richard Ammons, from the county public defender's office, was assigned on the day of arraignment as Brillon's first counsel. In October, Ammons filed a motion to recuse the trial judge. It was denied the next month and trial was scheduled for February 2002. In mid-January, Ammons moved for a continuance, but the State objected, and the trial court denied the motion.

On February 22, four days before the jury draw, Ammons again moved for a continuance, citing his heavy workload and the need for further investigation. Ammons acknowledged that any delay would not count (presumably against the State) for speedy-trial purposes. The State opposed the motion, and at the conclusion of a hearing, the trial court denied it. Brillon, participating in the proceedings through interactive television, then announced: "You're fired, Rick." Three days later, the trial court—over the State's objection—granted Ammons' motion to withdraw as counsel, citing Brillon's termination of Ammons and Ammons' statement that he could no longer zealously represent Brillon.[3] The trial court warned Brillon that further delay would occur while a new attorney became familiar with the case. The same day, the trial court appointed a second attorney, but he immediately withdrew based on a conflict.

On March 1, 2002, Gerard Altieri was assigned as Brillon's third counsel. On May 20, Brillon filed a motion to dismiss Altieri for, among other reasons, failure to file motions, "[v]irtually no communication whatsoever," and his lack of diligence "because of heavy case load." At a June 11 hearing, Altieri denied several of Brillon's allegations, noted his disagreement with Brillon's trial strategy, and insisted he had plenty of time to prepare. The State opposed Brillon's motion as well. Near the end of the hearing, however, Altieri moved to withdraw on the ground that Brillon had threatened his life during a break in the proceedings. The trial court granted Brillon's motion to dismiss Altieri, but warned Brillon that "this is somewhat of a dubious victory in your case because it simply prolongs the time that you will remain in jail until we can bring this matter to trial."

That same day, the trial court appointed Paul Donaldson as Brillon's fourth counsel. At an August 5 status conference, Donaldson requested additional time to conduct discovery in light of his caseload. A few weeks later, Brillon sent a letter to the court complaining about Donaldson's unresponsiveness and lack of competence. Two months later, Brillon filed a motion to dismiss Donaldson—similar to his motion to dismiss Altieri—for failure to file motions and "virtually no communication whatsoever." At a November 26 hearing, Donaldson reported that his contract with the Defender General's office had expired in June and that he had been in discussions to have Brillon's case reassigned. The trial court released Donaldson from the case "[w]ithout making any findings regarding the adequacy of [Donaldson]'s representation."

Brillon's fifth counsel, David Sleigh, was not assigned until January 15, 2003; Brillon was without counsel during the intervening two months. On February 25, Sleigh sought extensions of various discovery deadlines, noting that he had been in trial out of town. On April 10, however, Sleigh withdrew from the case, based on "modifications to [his] firm's contract with the Defender General."

Brillon was then without counsel for the next four months. On June 20, the Defender General's office notified the court that it had received "funding from the legislature" and would hire a new special felony unit defender for Brillon. On August 1, Kathleen Moore was appointed as Brillon's sixth counsel. The trial court set November 7 as the deadline for motions, but granted several extensions in accord with the parties' stipulation. On February 23, 2004, Moore filed a motion to dismiss for lack of a speedy trial. The trial court denied the motion on April 19.

The case finally went to trial on June 14, 2004. Brillon was found guilty and sentenced to 12 to 20 years in prison. The trial court denied a post-trial motion to dismiss for want of a speedy trial, concluding that the delay in Brillon's trial was "in large part the result of his own actions" and that Brillon had "failed to demonstrate prejudice as a result of [the] pre-trial delay."

II

The *Sixth Amendment* guarantees that "[i]n all criminal prosecutions, the accused shall enjoy the right to a speedy . . . trial." The speedy-trial right is "amorphous," "slippery," and "necessarily relative." In *Barker*, the Court refused to "quantif[y]" the right "into a specified number of days or months" or to hinge the right on a defendant's explicit request for a speedy trial. Rejecting such "inflexible approaches," *Barker* established a "balancing test, in which the conduct of both the prosecution and the defendant are weighed." "[S]ome of the factors" that courts should weigh include "[l]ength of delay, the reason for the delay, the defendant's assertion of his right, and prejudice to the defendant."

Primarily at issue here is the reason for the delay in Brillon's trial. Because "the attorney is the [defendant's] agent when acting, or failing to act, in furtherance of the litigation," delay caused by the defendant's counsel is also charged against the defendant. The same principle applies whether counsel is privately retained or publicly assigned, for "[o]nce a lawyer has undertaken the representation of an accused, the duties and obligations are the same whether the lawyer is privately retained, appointed, or serving in a legal aid or defender program."

III

An assigned counsel's failure "to move the case forward" does not warrant attribution of delay to the State. Contrary to the Vermont Supreme Court's analysis, assigned counsel generally are not state actors for purposes of a speedy-trial claim. While the Vermont Defender General's office is indeed "part of the criminal justice system," the individual counsel here acted only on behalf of Brillon, not the State. Most of the delay that the Vermont Supreme Court attributed to the State must therefore be attributed to Brillon as delays caused by his counsel.

A contrary conclusion could encourage appointed counsel to delay proceedings by seeking unreasonable continuances, hoping thereby to obtain a dismissal of the indictment on speedy-trial grounds. Trial courts might well respond by viewing continuance requests made by appointed counsel with skepticism, concerned that even an apparently genuine need for more time is in reality a delay tactic.

The general rule attributing to the defendant delay caused by assigned counsel is not absolute. Delay resulting from a systemic "breakdown in the public defender system," could be charged to the State. But the Vermont Supreme Court made no determination, and nothing in the record suggests, that institutional problems caused any part of the delay in Brillon's case.

In sum, delays caused by defense counsel are properly attributed to the defendant, even where counsel is assigned.

Chapter 11

RIGHT TO COUNSEL

B.   When the Right to Counsel Applies (casebook page 698)

In *Rothgery v. Gillespie County*, the Court reaffirmed that the Sixth Amendment right to counsel attaches at the defendant's first appearance before a judicial officer after a formal charge is made, regardless of whether a prosecutor is present. The first appearance triggers the "adversarial process" that entitles the defendant to the right to counsel.

Rothgery v. Gillespie County
128 S.Ct. 2578 (2008)

Justice SOUTER delivered the opinion of the Court.

This Court has held that the right to counsel guaranteed by the *Sixth Amendment* applies at the first appearance before a judicial officer at which a defendant is told of the formal accusation against him and restrictions are imposed on his liberty. See *Brewer v. Williams* (1977); *Michigan v. Jackson* (1986). The question here is whether attachment of the right also requires that a public prosecutor (as distinct from a police officer) be aware of that initial proceeding or involved in its conduct. We hold that it does not.

Although petitioner Walter Rothgery has never been convicted of a felony, a criminal background check disclosed an erroneous record that he had been, and on July 15, 2002, Texas police officers relied on this record to arrest him as a felon in possession of a firearm. The officers lacked a warrant, and so promptly brought Rothgery before a magistrate judge, as required by [Texas law]. Texas law has no formal label for this initial appearance before a magistrate, which is sometimes called the "article 15.17 hearing." [I]t combines the *Fourth Amendment's* required probable-cause determination with the setting of bail, and is the point at which the arrestee is formally apprised of the accusation against him.

Rothgery's article 15.17 hearing followed routine. The arresting officer submitted a sworn "Affidavit Of Probable Cause" that described the facts supporting the arrest and "charge[d] that . . . Rothgery . . . commit[ted] the offense of unlawful possession of a firearm by a felon—3rd degree felony After reviewing the affidavit, the magistrate judge "determined that probable cause existed for the arrest." The magistrate judge informed Rothgery of the accusation, set his bail at $ 5,000, and committed him to jail, from which he was released after posting a surety bond.

Rothgery had no money for a lawyer and made several oral and written requests for appointed counsel, which went unheeded. The following January, he was indicted by a Texas grand jury for unlawful possession of a firearm by a felon, resulting in rearrest the next day, and an order increasing bail to $ 15,000. When he could not post it, he was put in jail and remained there for three weeks.

On January 23, 2003, six months after the article 15.17 hearing, Rothgery was finally assigned a lawyer, who promptly obtained a bail reduction (so Rothgery could get out of jail), and assembled the paperwork confirming that Rothgery had never been convicted of a felony. Counsel relayed this information to the district attorney, who in turn filed a motion to dismiss the indictment, which was granted.

Rothgery then brought this *42 U.S.C. §1983* action against respondent Gillespie County, claiming that if the County had provided a lawyer within a reasonable time after the article 15.17 hearing, he would not have been indicted, rearrested, or jailed for three weeks. The County's failure is said to be owing to its unwritten policy of denying appointed counsel to indigent defendants out on bond until at least the entry of an information or indictment. Rothgery sees this policy as violating his *Sixth Amendment* right to counsel.

The *Sixth Amendment* right of the "accused" to assistance of counsel in "all criminal prosecutions" is limited by its terms: "it does not attach until a prosecution is commenced." We have, for purposes of the right to counsel, pegged commencement to " 'the initiation of adversary judicial criminal proceedings — whether by way of formal charge, preliminary hearing, indictment, information, or arraignment.' " The rule is not "mere formalism," but a recognition of the point at which "the government has committed itself to prosecute," "the adverse positions of government and defendant have solidified," and the accused "finds himself faced with the prosecutorial forces of organized society, and immersed in the intricacies of substantive and procedural criminal law." The issue is whether Texas's article 15.17 hearing marks that point, with the consequent state obligation to appoint counsel within a reasonable time once a request for assistance is made.

When the Court of Appeals said no, because no prosecutor was aware of Rothgery's article 15.17 hearing or involved in it, the court effectively focused not on the start of adversarial judicial proceedings, but on the activities and knowledge of a particular state official who was presumably otherwise occupied. This was error.

As the Court of Appeals recognized, we have twice held that the right to counsel attaches at the initial appearance before a judicial officer, see *Michigan v. Jackson* (1986); *Brewer v. Williams* (1977). Neither *Brewer* nor *Jackson* said a word about the prosecutor's involvement as a relevant fact, much less a controlling one. [A]n attachment rule that turned on determining the moment of a prosecutor's first involvement would be "wholly unworkable and impossible to administer," guaranteed to bog the courts down in prying enquiries into the communication between police (who are routinely present at defendants' first appearances) and the State's attorneys (who are not).

Our holding is narrow. We do not decide whether the 6-month delay in appointment of counsel resulted in prejudice to Rothgery's *Sixth Amendment* rights, and have no occasion to consider what standards should apply in deciding this. We merely reaffirm what we have held before and what an overwhelming majority of American jurisdictions understand in practice: a criminal defendant's initial appearance before a judicial officer, where he learns the charge against him and his liberty is subject to restriction, marks the start of adversary judicial proceedings that trigger attachment of the *Sixth Amendment* right to counsel.

Justice THOMAS, dissenting.

The Court holds today—for the first time after plenary consideration of the question—that a criminal prosecution begins, and that the *Sixth Amendment* right to counsel therefore attaches, when an individual who has been placed under arrest makes an initial appearance before a magistrate for a probable-cause determination and the setting of bail. Because the Court's holding is not supported by the original meaning of the *Sixth Amendment* or any reasonable interpretation of our precedents, I respectfully dissent.

Blackstone thus provides a definition of "prosecution": the manner of an offender's "formal accusation." The modifier "formal" is significant because it distinguishes "prosecution" from earlier stages of the process involving a different kind of accusation: the allegation of criminal conduct necessary to justify arrest and detention.

By "formal accusation," Blackstone meant, in most cases, "indictment, the most usual and effectual means of prosecution." The affidavit of probable cause clearly was not the type of formal accusation Blackstone identified with the commencement of a criminal "prosecution." Rather, it was the preliminary accusation necessary to justify arrest and detention—stages of the criminal process that Blackstone placed before prosecution.

Neither petitioner nor the Court identifies any way in which petitioner's ability to receive a fair trial was undermined by the absence of counsel during the period between his initial appearance and his indictment. Nothing during that period exposed petitioner to the risk that he would be convicted as the result of ignorance of his rights. Instead, the gravamen of petitioner's complaint is that if counsel had been appointed earlier, he would have been able to stave off indictment by convincing the prosecutor that petitioner was not guilty of the crime alleged. But the *Sixth Amendment* protects against the risk of erroneous *conviction*, not the risk of unwarranted *prosecution*.

E.   Right of Self-Representation (casebook page 727)

In *Indiana v. Edwards*, the Court addressed an issue left open by *Faretta*: Is a defendant who is competent to stand trial necessarily competent enough to represent himself at trial? Unlike the Court's ruling in *Godinez v. Moran* (1993), which rejected a higher standard of competency for a pro se defendant to plead guilty, the Court in *Indiana v. Edwards* held that courts may impose a heightened competency standard for a defendant who wants to represent himself at trial.

Indiana v. Edwards
128 S.Ct. 2379 (2008)

Justice BREYER delivered the opinion of the Court.

This case focuses upon a criminal defendant whom a state court found mentally competent to stand trial if represented by counsel but not mentally competent to conduct that trial himself. We must decide whether in these circumstances the Constitution forbids a State from insisting that the defendant proceed to trial with counsel, the State thereby denying the defendant the right to represent himself. We conclude that the Constitution does not forbid a State so to insist.

I

In July 1999 Ahmad Edwards, the respondent, tried to steal a pair of shoes from an Indiana department store. After he was discovered, he drew a gun, fired at a store security officer, and wounded a bystander. He was caught and then charged with attempted murder, battery with a deadly weapon, criminal recklessness, and theft. His mental condition subsequently became the subject of three competency proceedings and two self-representation requests, mostly before the same trial judge:

First Competency Hearing: August 2000. Five months after Edwards' arrest, his court-appointed counsel asked for a psychiatric evaluation. After hearing psychiatrist and neuropsychologist witnesses (in February 2000 and again in August 2000), the court found Edwards incompetent to stand trial, and committed him to Logansport State Hospital for evaluation and treatment.

Second Competency Hearing: March 2002. Seven months after his commitment, doctors found that Edwards' condition had improved to the point where he could stand trial. Several months later, however, but still before trial, Edwards' counsel asked for another psychiatric evaluation. In March 2002, the judge held a competency hearing, considered additional psychiatric evidence, and (in April) found that Edwards, while "suffer[ing] from mental illness," was "competent to assist his attorneys in his defense and stand trial for the charged crimes."

Third Competency Hearing: April 2003. Seven months later but still before trial, Edwards' counsel sought yet another psychiatric evaluation of his client. And, in April 2003, the court held yet another competency hearing. Edwards' counsel presented further psychiatric and neuropsychological evidence showing that Edwards was suffering from serious thinking difficulties and delusions. A testifying psychiatrist reported that Edwards could understand the charges against him, but he was "unable to cooperate with his attorney in his defense because of his schizophrenic illness"; "[h]is delusions and his marked difficulties in thinking make it impossible for him to cooperate with his attorney." In November 2003, the court concluded that Edwards was not then competent to stand trial and ordered his recommitment to the state hospital.

First Self-Representation Request and First Trial: June 2005. About eight months after his commitment, the hospital reported that Edwards' condition had again improved to the point that he had again become competent to stand trial. And almost one year after that Edwards' trial began. Just before trial, Edwards asked to represent himself. He also asked for a continuance, which, he said, he needed in order to proceed *pro se.* The court refused the continuance. Edwards then proceeded to trial represented by counsel. The jury convicted him of criminal recklessness and theft but failed to reach a verdict on the charges of attempted murder and battery.

Second Self-Representation Request and Second Trial: December 2005. The State decided to retry Edwards on the attempted murder and battery charges. Just before the retrial, Edwards again asked the court to permit him to represent himself. Referring to the lengthy record of psychiatric reports, the trial court noted that Edwards still suffered from schizophrenia and concluded that "[w]ith these findings, he's competent to stand trial but I'm not going to find he's competent to defend himself." The court denied Edwards' self-representation request. Edwards was represented by appointed counsel at his retrial. The jury convicted Edwards on both of the remaining counts.

II

Our examination of this Court's precedents convinces us that those precedents frame the question presented, but they do not answer it. *Dusky* defines the competency standard as including both (1) "whether" the defendant has "a rational as well as factual understanding of the proceedings against him" and (2) whether the defendant "has sufficient present ability *to consult with his lawyer* with a reasonable degree of rational understanding." [Neither *Dusky* nor any other prior case, including *Faretta*] considered the mental competency issue presented here, namely, the relation of the mental competence standard to the right of self-representation.

The sole case in which this Court considered mental competence and self-representation together, *Godinez* (1993), presents a question closer to that at issue here. The case focused upon a borderline-competent criminal defendant who had asked a state trial court to permit him to represent himself and to change his pleas from not guilty to guilty. This Court, reversing the Court of Appeals, "reject[ed] the notion that competence to plead guilty or to waive the right to counsel must be measured by a standard that is higher than (or even different from) the *Dusky* standard."

We concede that *Godinez* bears certain similarities with the present case. Both involve mental competence and self-representation. Both involve a defendant who wants to represent himself. Both involve a mental condition that falls in a gray area between *Dusky*'s minimal constitutional requirement that measures a defendant's ability to stand trial and a somewhat higher standard that measures mental fitness for another legal purpose.

We nonetheless conclude that *Godinez* does not answer the question before us now. *Godinez* defendant sought only to change his pleas to guilty, he did not seek to conduct trial proceedings, and his ability to conduct a defense at trial was expressly not at issue.

We now turn to the question presented. We assume that a criminal defendant has sufficient mental competence to stand trial (*i.e.*, the defendant meets *Dusky*'s standard) and that the defendant insists on representing himself during that trial. We ask whether the Constitution permits a State to limit that defendant's self-representation right by insisting upon representation by counsel at trial—on the ground that the defendant lacks the mental capacity to conduct his trial defense unless represented.

Several considerations taken together lead us to conclude that the answer to this question is yes. First, an instance in which a defendant who would choose to forgo counsel at trial presents a very different set of circumstances, which in our view, calls for a different standard.

Second, the nature of the problem before us cautions against the use of a single mental competency standard for deciding both (1) whether a defendant who is represented by counsel can proceed to trial and (2) whether a defendant who goes to trial must be permitted to represent himself. Mental illness itself is not a unitary concept. It varies in degree. It can vary over time. It interferes with an individual's functioning at different times in different ways. The history of this case illustrates the complexity of the problem. In certain instances an individual may well be able to satisfy *Dusky*'s mental competence standard, for he will be able to work with counsel at trial, yet at the same time he may be unable to carry out the basic tasks needed to present his own defense without the help of counsel.

Third, in our view, a right of self-representation at trial will not "affirm the dignity" of a defendant who lacks the mental capacity to conduct his defense without the assistance of counsel. To the contrary, given that defendant's uncertain mental state, the spectacle that could well result from his self-representation at trial is at least as likely to prove humiliating as ennobling. Moreover, insofar as a defendant's lack of capacity threatens an improper conviction or sentence, self-representation in that exceptional context undercuts the most basic of the Constitution's criminal law objectives, providing a fair trial.

Further, proceedings must not only be fair, they must "appear fair to all who observe them." An *amicus* brief reports one psychiatrist's reaction to having observed a patient (a patient who had satisfied *Dusky*) try to conduct his own defense: "[H]ow in the world can our legal system allow an insane man to defend himself?"

We consequently conclude that the Constitution permits judges to take realistic account of the particular defendant's mental capacities by asking whether a defendant who seeks to conduct his own defense at trial is mentally competent to do so. That is to say, the Constitution permits States to insist upon representation by counsel for those competent enough to stand trial under *Dusky* but who still suffer from severe mental illness to the point where they are not competent to conduct trial proceedings by themselves.

Indiana has also asked us to adopt, as a measure of a defendant's ability to conduct a trial, a more specific standard that would "deny a criminal defendant the right to represent himself at trial where the defendant cannot communicate coherently with the court or a jury." We are sufficiently uncertain, however, as to how that particular standard would work in practice to refrain from endorsing it as a federal constitutional standard here. We need not now, and we do not, adopt it.

Indiana has also asked us to overrule *Faretta*. We decline to do so. We recognize that judges have sometimes expressed concern that *Faretta*, contrary to its intent, has led to trials that are unfair. But recent empirical research suggests that such instances are not common. See, *e.g.*, Hashimoto, *Defending the Right of Self-Representation: An Empirical Look at the Pro Se Felony Defendant*, 85 N. C. L. Rev. 423, 427, 447, 428 (2007) (noting that of the small number of defendants who chose to proceed *pro se*—"roughly 0.3% to 0.5%" of the total, state felony defendants in particular "appear to have achieved higher felony acquittal rates than their represented counterparts in that they were less likely to have been convicted of felonies").

For these reasons, the judgment of the Supreme Court of Indiana is vacated, and the case is remanded for further proceedings not inconsistent with this opinion.

Justice SCALIA, with whom Justice THOMAS joins, dissenting.

The Constitution guarantees a defendant who knowingly and voluntarily waives the right to counsel the right to proceed *pro se* at his trial. *Faretta v. California* (1975). A mentally ill defendant who knowingly and voluntarily elects to proceed *pro se* instead of through counsel receives a fair trial that comports with the *Fourteenth Amendment*. The Court today concludes that a State may nonetheless strip a mentally ill defendant of the right to represent himself when that would be fairer. In my view the Constitution does not permit a State to substitute its own perception of fairness for the defendant's right to make his own case before the jury—a specific right long understood as essential to a fair trial.

Over the course of what became two separate criminal trials, Edwards sought to act as his own lawyer. He filed a number of incoherent written pleadings with the judge on which the Court places emphasis, but he also filed several intelligible pleadings, such as a motion to dismiss counsel, a motion to dismiss charges under the Indiana speedy trial provision, and a motion seeking a trial transcript.

Edwards made arguments in the courtroom that were more coherent than his written pleadings. In seeking to represent himself at his first trial, Edwards complained in detail that the attorney representing him had not spent adequate time preparing and was not sharing legal materials for use in his defense. The trial judge concluded that Edwards had knowingly and voluntarily waived his right to counsel and proceeded to quiz Edwards about matters of state law. Edwards correctly answered questions about the meaning of *voir dire* and how it operated, and described the basic framework for admitting videotape evidence to trial, though he was unable to answer other questions, including questions about the topics covered by state evidentiary rules that the judge identified only by number. He persisted in his request to represent himself, but the judge denied the request because Edwards acknowledged he would need a continuance. Represented by counsel, he was convicted of criminal recklessness and theft, but the jury deadlocked on charges of attempted murder and battery.

At his second trial, Edwards again asked the judge to be allowed to proceed *pro se*. He explained that he and his attorney disagreed about which defense to present to the attempted murder charge.

The court again rejected Edwards' request to proceed *pro se*, and this time it did not have the justification that Edwards had sought a continuance. The court did not dispute that Edwards knowingly and intelligently waived his right to counsel, but stated it was "going to carve out a third exception" to the right of self-representation, and—without explaining precisely what abilities Edwards lacked—stated Edwards was "competent to stand trial but I'm not going to find he's competent to defend himself."

The Constitution guarantees to every criminal defendant the "right to proceed *without* counsel when he voluntarily and intelligently elects to do so." The right reflects "a nearly universal conviction, on the part of our people as well as our courts, that forcing a lawyer upon an unwilling defendant is contrary to his basic right to defend himself if he truly wants to do so." *Faretta*'s discussion of the history of the right, includes the observation that "[i]n the long history of British criminal jurisprudence, there was only one tribunal that ever adopted a practice of forcing counsel upon an unwilling defendant in a criminal proceeding. The tribunal was the Star Chamber." *Faretta* described the right to proceed *pro se* as a premise of the *Sixth Amendment*, which confers the tools for a defense on the "accused," and describes the role of the attorney as one of "assistance." The right of self-representation could also be seen as a part of the traditional meaning of the *Due Process Clause*. Whichever provision provides its source, it means that a State simply may not force a lawyer upon a criminal defendant who wishes to conduct his own defense.

When a defendant appreciates the risks of forgoing counsel and chooses to do so voluntarily, the Constitution protects his ability to present his own defense even when that harms his case. In fact waiving counsel "usually" does so. We have nonetheless said that the defendant's "choice must be honored out of 'that respect for the individual which is the lifeblood of the law.'" What the Constitution requires is not that a State's case be subject to the most rigorous adversarial testing possible—after all, it permits a defendant to eliminate *all* adversarial testing by pleading guilty. What the Constitution requires is that a defendant be given the right to challenge the State's case against him using the arguments *he* sees fit.

Until today, the right of self-representation has been accorded the same respect as other constitutional guarantees. The only circumstance in which we have permitted the State to deprive a defendant of this trial right is the one under which we have allowed the State to deny *other* such rights: when it is necessary to enable the trial to proceed in an orderly fashion. That overriding necessity, we have said, justifies forfeiture of even the *Sixth Amendment* right to be present at trial—if, after being threatened with removal, a defendant "insists on conducting himself in a manner so disorderly, disruptive, and disrespectful of the court that his trial cannot be carried on with him in the courtroom." A *pro se* defendant may not "abuse the dignity of the courtroom," nor may he fail to "comply with relevant rules of procedural and substantive law," and a court may "terminate" the self-representation of a defendant who "deliberately engages in serious and obstructionist misconduct." This ground for terminating self-representation is unavailable here, however, because Edwards was not even allowed to begin to represent himself, and because he was respectful and compliant and did not provide a basis to conclude a trial could not have gone forward had he been allowed to press his own claims.

I believe the Court's assessment of the purposes of the right of self-representation is inaccurate to boot. While there is little doubt that preserving individual " 'dignity' " (to which the Court refers), is paramount among those purposes, there is equally little doubt that the loss of "dignity" the right is designed to prevent is *not* the defendant's making a fool of himself by presenting an amateurish or even incoherent defense. Rather, the dignity at issue is the supreme human dignity of being master of one's fate rather than a ward of the State—the dignity of individual choice. In sum, if the Court is to honor the particular conception of "dignity" that underlies the self-representation right, it should respect the autonomy of the individual by honoring his choices knowingly and voluntarily made.

The facts of this case illustrate this point with the utmost clarity. Edwards wished to take a self-defense case to the jury. His counsel preferred a defense that focused on lack of intent. Having been denied the right to conduct his own defense, Edwards was convicted without having had the opportunity to present to the jury the grounds he believed supported his innocence. I do not doubt that he likely would have been convicted anyway. But to hold that a defendant may be deprived of the right to make legal arguments for acquittal simply because a state-selected agent has made different arguments on his behalf is, as Justice Frankfurter wrote, to "imprison a man in his privileges and call it the Constitution." In singling out mentally ill defendants for this treatment, the Court's opinion does not even have the questionable virtue of being politically correct. At a time when all society is trying to mainstream the mentally impaired, the Court permits them to be deprived of a basic constitutional right—for their own good.

Today's holding is extraordinarily vague. The Court does not accept Indiana's position that self-representation can be denied "'where the defendant cannot communicate coherently with the court or a jury,'" It does not even hold that Edwards was properly denied his right to represent himself. It holds only that lack of mental competence can under some circumstances form a basis for denying the right to proceed *pro se*. We will presumably give some meaning to this holding in the future, but the indeterminacy makes a bad holding worse. Once the right of self-representation for the mentally ill is a sometime thing, trial judges will have every incentive to make their lives easier—to avoid the painful necessity of deciphering occasional pleadings by appointing knowledgeable and literate counsel.

Because I think a defendant who is competent to stand trial, and who is capable of knowing and voluntary waiver of assistance of counsel, has a constitutional right to conduct his own defense, I respectfully dissent.

Chapter 12

TRIAL

B. Jury Composition and Selection

3. Applying Batson

e. *The Mechanics of Bringing* Batson *Challenges (casebook page 766)*

In *Miller-El v. Dretke* (2005), the Court indicated that it would look to the entire record of jury selection to determine the validity of a proffered race-neutral reason for challenging a juror. When it did so in *Synder v. Louisiana*, it determined that the trial court had erred in accepting the prosecutor's explanation and that even the improper challenge of one juror requires a new trial.

Snyder v. Louisiana
128 S.Ct. 1203 (2008)

Justice ALITO delivered the opinion of the Court.

Petitioner Allen Snyder was convicted of first-degree murder in a Louisiana court and was sentenced to death. He asks us to review a decision of the Louisiana Supreme Court rejecting his claim that the prosecution exercised some of its peremptory jury challenges based on race, in violation of *Batson v. Kentucky* (1986). We hold that the trial court committed clear error in its ruling on a *Batson* objection, and we therefore reverse.

The crime for which petitioner was convicted [of murdering his estranged wife].

Eighty-five prospective jurors were questioned as members of a panel. Thirty-six of these survived challenges for cause; 5 of the 36 were black; and all 5 of the prospective black jurors were eliminated by the prosecution through the use of peremptory strikes. The jury found petitioner guilty of first-degree murder and determined that he should receive the death penalty.

Batson provides a three-step process for a trial court to use in adjudicating a claim that a peremptory challenge was based on race:

"'First, a defendant must make a prima facie showing that a peremptory challenge has been exercised on the basis of race[; s]econd, if that showing has been made, the prosecution must offer a race-neutral basis for striking the juror in question[; and t]hird, in light of the parties' submissions, the trial court must determine whether the defendant has shown purposeful discrimination.'" *Miller-El v. Dretke* (2005).

Petitioner centers his *Batson* claim on the prosecution's strikes of two black jurors, Jeffrey Brooks and Elaine Scott. Because we find that the trial court committed clear error in overruling petitioner's *Batson* objection with respect to Mr. Brooks, we have no need to consider petitioner's claim regarding Ms. Scott.

In *Miller-El v. Dretke*, the Court made it clear that in considering a *Batson* objection, or in reviewing a ruling claimed to be *Batson* error, all of the circumstances that bear upon the issue of racial animosity must be consulted. In this case, . . . the explanation given for the strike of Mr. Brooks is by itself unconvincing and suffices for the determination that there was *Batson* error.

When defense counsel made a *Batson* objection concerning the strike of Mr. Brooks, a college senior who was attempting to fulfill his student-teaching obligation, the prosecution offered two race-neutral reasons for the strike. The prosecutor explained:

> "I thought about it last night. Number 1, the main reason is that he looked very nervous to me throughout the questioning. Number 2, he's one of the fellows that came up at the beginning [of *voir dire*] and said he was going to miss class. He's a student teacher. My main concern is for that reason, that being that he might, to go home quickly, come back with guilty of a lesser verdict so there wouldn't be a penalty phase. Those are my two reasons."

With respect to the first reason, deference is especially appropriate where a trial judge has made a finding that an attorney credibly relied on demeanor in exercising a strike. Here, however, the record does not show that the trial judge actually made a determination concerning Mr. Brooks' demeanor.

The second reason proffered for the strike of Mr. Brooks—his student-teaching obligation—fails even under the highly deferential standard of review that is applicable here. At the beginning of *voir dire*, when the trial court asked the members of the venire whether jury service or sequestration would pose an extreme hardship, Mr. Brooks was 1 of more than 50 members of the venire who expressed concern that jury service or sequestration would interfere with work, school, family, or other obligations.

When Mr. Brooks came forward, the following exchange took place:

> "MR. JEFFREY BROOKS: . . . I'm a student at Southern University, New Orleans. This is my last semester. My major requires me to student teach, and today I've already missed a half a day. That is part of my—it's required for me to graduate this semester.
>
> "[DEFENSE COUNSEL]: Mr. Brooks, if you—how many days would you miss if you were sequestered on this jury? Do you teach every day?
>
> "MR. JEFFREY BROOKS: Five days a week.
>
> "[DEFENSE COUNSEL]: Five days a week.
>
> "MR. JEFFREY BROOKS: And it's 8:30 through 3:00.

"[DEFENSE COUNSEL]: If you missed this week, is there any way that you could make it up this [***15] semester?

"MR. JEFFREY BROOKS: Well, the first two weeks I observe, the remaining I begin teaching, so there is something I'm missing right now that will better me towards my teaching career.

"[DEFENSE COUNSEL]: Is there any way that you could make up the observed observation [sic] that you're missing today, at another time?

"MR. JEFFREY BROOKS: It may be possible, I'm not sure.

"[DEFENSE COUNSEL]: Okay. So that—

"THE COURT: Is there anyone we could call, like a Dean or anything, that we could speak to?

[*1210] "MR. JEFFREY BROOKS: Actually, I spoke to my Dean, Doctor Tillman, who's at the university probably right now.

"THE COURT: All right.

"MR. JEFFREY BROOKS: Would you like to speak to him?

"THE COURT: Yeah.

"MR. JEFFREY BROOKS: I don't have his card on me.

"THE COURT: Why don't you give [a law clerk] his number, give [a law clerk] his name and we'll call him and we'll see what we can do.

"(MR. JEFFREY BROOKS LEFT THE BENCH)."

Shortly thereafter, the court again spoke with Mr. Brooks:

"THE LAW CLERK: Jeffrey Brooks, the requirement for his teaching is a three hundred clock hour observation. Doctor Tillman at Southern University said that as long as it's just this week, he doesn't see that it would cause a problem with Mr. Brooks completing his observation time within this semester.

"THE COURT: We talked to Doctor Tillman and he says he doesn't see a problem as long as it's just this week, you know, he'll work with you on it. Okay?

"MR. JEFFREY BROOKS: Okay."

Once Mr. Brooks heard the law clerk's report about the conversation with Doctor Tillman, Mr. Brooks did not express any further concern about serving on the jury, and the prosecution did not choose to question him more deeply about this matter.

The prosecutor's second proffered reason for striking Mr. Brooks must be evaluated in light of these circumstances. The prosecutor claimed to be apprehensive that Mr. Brooks, in order to minimize the student-teaching hours missed during jury service, might have been motivated to find petitioner guilty, not of first-degree murder, but of a lesser included offense because this would obviate the need for a penalty phase proceeding. But this scenario was highly speculative. Even if Mr. Brooks had favored a quick resolution, that would not have necessarily led him to reject a finding of first-degree murder. If the majority of jurors had initially favored a finding of first-degree murder, Mr. Brooks' purported inclination might have led him to agree in order to speed the deliberations. Only if all or most of the other jurors had favored the lesser verdict would Mr. Brooks have been in a position to shorten the trial by favoring such a verdict.

The implausibility of this explanation is reinforced by the prosecutor's acceptance of white jurors who disclosed conflicting obligations that appear to have been at least as serious as Mr. Brooks'. We recognize that a retrospective comparison of jurors based on a cold appellate record may be very misleading when alleged similarities were not raised at trial. In that situation, an appellate court must be mindful that an exploration of the alleged similarities at the time of trial might have shown that the jurors in question were not really comparable. In this case, however, the shared characteristic, *i.e.*, concern about serving on the jury due to conflicting obligations, was thoroughly explored by the trial court when the relevant jurors asked to be excused for cause.

A comparison between Mr. Brooks and Roland Laws, a white juror, is particularly striking. During the initial stage of *voir dire*, Mr. Laws approached the court and offered strong reasons why serving on the sequestered jury would cause him hardship. Mr. Laws stated that he was "a self-employed general contractor," with "two houses that are nearing completion, one [with the occupants] . . . moving in this weekend." Mr. Laws also had demanding family obligations:

> "[M]y wife just had a hysterectomy, so I'm running the kids back and forth to school, and we're not originally from here, so I have no family in the area, so between the two things, it's kind of bad timing for me."

Although these obligations seem substantially more pressing than Mr. Brooks', the prosecution questioned Mr. Laws and attempted to elicit assurances that he would be able to serve despite his work and family obligations. And the prosecution declined the opportunity to use a peremptory strike on Mr. Laws. If the prosecution had been sincerely concerned that Mr. Brooks would favor a lesser verdict than first-degree murder in order to shorten the trial, it is hard to see why the prosecution would not have had at least as much concern regarding Mr. Laws.

As previously noted, the question presented at the third stage of the *Batson* inquiry is "'whether the defendant has shown purposeful discrimination.'" The prosecution's proffer of this pretextual explanation naturally gives rise to an inference of discriminatory intent.

We therefore reverse the judgment.

Justice THOMAS, with whom Justice SCALIA joins, dissenting.

The Court's conclusion, however, reveals that it is only paying lipservice to the pivotal role of the trial court. The Court second-guesses the trial court's determinations in this case merely because the judge did not clarify which of the prosecutor's neutral bases for striking Mr. Brooks was dispositive.

The prosecution offered two neutral bases for striking Mr. Brooks: his nervous demeanor and his stated concern about missing class. The trial court, in rejecting defendant's *Batson* challenge, stated only "All right. I'm going to allow the challenge. I'm going to allow the challenge." Given the trial court's expertise in making credibility determinations and its firsthand knowledge of the *voir dire* exchanges, it is entirely proper to defer to its judgment. Accordingly, I would affirm the judgment below.

* * *

In *Rivera v. Illinois*, 129 S.Ct. 1446 (2009), the Supreme Court held that even if a judge erroneously seats a juror who should have been dismissed under a proper use of a peremptory challenge, the defendant is not entitled to reversal of the conviction. There is no Due Process violation so long as all seated jurors are qualified and unbiased.

D. Trial Rights: Due Process, Right of Confrontation, and Privilege Against Self-Incrimination (casebook page 803)

In *Melendez-Diaz v. Massachusetts*, 129 S.Ct. _____ (2009), Justice Alito continued to define the scope of *Crawford*. Writing for a 5-4 majority, he held that affidavits by forensic specialists constitute testimonial evidence and therefore violate a defendant's right of confrontation. If the prosecution wants to present the laboratory results that show a tested drug was contraband, it must call the analyst who conducted the test, unless the defendant has waived this right.

Chapter 13

SENTENCING

B. Indeterminate Versus Determinate Sentencing

4. *Apprendi* and Its Progeny (casebook page 836)

Post-Booker, appellate courts review federal sentences for "reasonableness." Great deference is given to the sentencing court so long as the judge complied with the terms of 18 U.S.C. §3553(a). The appellate courts can strike down a sentence for being too excessive. However, unless the government cross-appeals, the appellate court cannot increase a sentence even if it believes that it was plainly wrong. In *Greenlaw v. United States*, 128 S.Ct. 2559 (2008), the Court held that it was up to the parties to frame the issues on appeal and the court will not "sally forth each day looking for wrongs to right." By reaching this result, the Supreme Court made it less risky for defendants to appeal their federal sentences.

In *Oregon v. Ice* (2009), the Court held that *Apprendi* does not extend to judges deciding facts that will determine whether a defendant receives a consecutive or concurrent sentence. Writing for a 5-4 majority, Justice Ginsburg held that the historical practice of having judges decide whether sentences will be consecutive or concurrent does not violate the Sixth Amendment.

Oregon v. Ice
129 S.Ct. 711 (2009)

Justice GINSBURG delivered the opinion of the Court.

This case concerns the scope of the *Sixth Amendment's* jury-trial guarantee, as construed in *Apprendi v. New Jersey* (2000), and *Blakely v. Washington* (2004). Those decisions are rooted in the historic jury function—determining whether the prosecution has proved each element of an offense beyond a reasonable doubt. They hold that it is within the jury's province to determine any fact (other than the existence of a prior conviction) that increases the maximum punishment authorized for a particular offense. Thus far, the Court has not extended the *Apprendi* and *Blakely* line of decisions beyond the offense-specific context that supplied the historic grounding for the decisions. The question here presented concerns a sentencing function in which the jury traditionally played no part: When a defendant has been tried and convicted of multiple offenses, each involving discrete sentencing prescriptions, does the *Sixth Amendment* mandate jury determination of any fact declared necessary to the imposition of consecutive, in lieu of concurrent, sentences?

Most States continue the common-law tradition: They entrust to judges' unfettered discretion the decision whether sentences for discrete offenses shall be served consecutively or concurrently. In some States, sentences for multiple offenses are presumed to run consecutively, but sentencing judges may order concurrent sentences upon finding cause therefor. Other States, including Oregon, constrain judges' discretion by requiring them to find certain facts before imposing consecutive, rather than concurrent, sentences. It is undisputed that States may proceed on the first two tracks without transgressing the *Sixth Amendment*. The sole issue in dispute, then, is whether the *Sixth Amendment*, as construed in *Apprendi* and *Blakely*, precludes the mode of proceeding chosen by Oregon and several of her sister States. We hold, in light of historical practice and the authority of States over administration of their criminal justice systems, that the *Sixth Amendment* does not exclude Oregon's choice.

I

State laws, as just observed, prescribe a variety of approaches to the decision whether a defendant's sentences for distinct offenses shall run concurrently or consecutively. Oregon might have followed the prevailing pattern by placing the decision within the trial court's discretion in all, or almost all, circumstances. Instead, Oregon and several other States have adopted a more restrained approach: they provide for judicial discretion, but constrain its exercise. In these States, to impose consecutive sentences, judges must make certain predicate fact findings.

Specifically, an Oregon judge may order consecutive sentences " [i]f a defendant is simultaneously sentenced for criminal offenses that do not arise from the same continuous and uninterrupted course of conduct." If the offenses *do* arise from the same course of conduct, the judge may still impose consecutive sentences if she finds either:

"(a)That the criminal offense ... was an indication of defendant's willingness to commit more than one criminal offense; or "(b) The criminal offense ... caused or created a risk of causing greater or qualitatively different loss, injury or harm to the victim or ... to a different victim. ... "

On two occasions between December 1996 and July 1997, respondent Thomas Eugene Ice entered an apartment in the complex he managed and sexually assaulted an 11-year-old girl. An Oregon jury convicted Ice of six crimes. For each of the two incidents, the jury found him guilty of first-degree burglary for entering with the intent to commit sexual abuse; first-degree sexual assault for touching the victim's vagina; and first-degree sexual assault for touching the victim's breasts.

At sentencing, the judge made findings ... that permitted the imposition of consecutive sentences. First, the judge found that the two burglaries constituted "separate incident[s]." Based on that finding, the judge had, and exercised, discretion to impose the two burglary sentences consecutively. Second, the court found that each offense of touching the victim's vagina met the statutory criteria: Ice displayed a "willingness to commit more than one ... offense" during each criminal episode, and his conduct "caused or created a risk of causing greater, qualitatively different loss, injury, or harm to the victim." These findings gave the judge discretion to impose the sentence for each of those sexual assault offenses consecutive to the associated burglary sentence. The court elected to do so. The court ordered, however, that the sentences for touching the victim's breasts run concurrently with the other sentences. In total, the court sentenced Ice to 340 months' imprisonment.[5]

II

The Federal Constitution's jury-trial guarantee assigns the determination of certain facts to the jury's exclusive province. Under that guarantee, this Court held in *Apprendi*, "any fact that increases the penalty for a crime beyond the prescribed statutory maximum must be submitted to a jury, and proved beyond a reasonable doubt."

We have applied *Apprendi*'s rule to facts subjecting a defendant to the death penalty, *Ring v. Arizona* (2002), facts allowing a sentence exceeding the "standard" range in Washington's sentencing system, *Blakely* (2004), and facts prompting an elevated sentence under then-mandatory Federal Sentencing Guidelines, *United States v. Booker*, (2005). Most recently, in *Cunningham v. California* (2007), we applied *Apprendi*'s rule to facts permitting imposition of an "upper term" sentence under California's determinate sentencing law. All of these decisions involved sentencing for a discrete crime, not—as here—for multiple offenses different in character or committed at different times.

Our application of *Apprendi*'s rule must honor the "long-standing common-law practice" in which the rule is rooted. The rule's animating principle is the preservation of the jury's historic role as a bulwark between the State and the accused at the trial for an alleged offense. We accordingly considered whether the finding of a particular fact was understood as within "the domain of the jury . . . by those who framed the *Bill of Rights*."

The historical record demonstrates that the jury played no role in the decision to impose sentences consecutively or concurrently. Rather, the choice rested exclusively with the judge. This was so in England before the founding of our Nation,[8] and in the early American States.[9] The historical record further indicates that a judge's imposition of consecutive, rather than concurrent, sentences was the prevailing practice.[10]

States' interest in the development of their penal systems, and their historic dominion in this area, also counsel against the extension of *Apprendi* that Ice requests. Beyond question, the authority of States over the administration of their criminal justice systems lies at the core of their sovereign status. We have long recognized the role of the States as laboratories for devising solutions to difficult legal problems. This Court should not diminish that role absent impelling reason to do so.

---

5. Had the judge ordered concurrent service of all sentences, Ice's time in prison would have been 90 months.

Moreover, the expansion that Ice seeks would be difficult for States to administer. The predicate facts for consecutive sentences could substantially prejudice the defense at the guilt phase of a trial. As a result, bifurcated or trifurcated trials might often prove necessary. We will not so burden the Nation's trial courts absent any genuine affront to *Apprendi*'s instruction.

Justice Scalia, with whom The Chief Justice, Justice Souter, and Justice Thomas join, dissenting.

The rule of *Apprendi v. New Jersey* (2000) is clear: Any fact—other than that of a prior conviction—that increases the maximum punishment to which a defendant may be sentenced must be admitted by the defendant or proved beyond a reasonable doubt to a jury. Oregon's sentencing scheme allows judges rather than juries to find the facts necessary to commit defendants to longer prison sentences, and thus directly contradicts what we held eight years ago and have reaffirmed several times since. The Court's justification of Oregon's scheme is a virtual copy of the dissents in those cases.

D. The Death Penalty

2. Standards for Constitutional Implementation of the Death Penalty (casebook page 863)

In *Kennedy v. Louisiana*, 128 S.Ct. 2641 (2008), the Court further held that the death penalty is disproportionate for crimes involving sexual assault against minors. In an opinion by Justice Kennedy, the Court reiterated that capital punishment must "be limited to those offenders who commit 'a narrow category of the most serious crimes' and whose extreme culpability makes them 'the most deserving of execution.'" The Court then found a national consensus against the death penalty for child rape cases. Its decision was based in large part on the fact that only six states currently authorize the death penalty for child rape. (Interestingly, after the Court issued its decision, it was also discovered that federal military law also authorizes the death penalty in such cases.) The court found that the death penalty for child rape does not meet "evolving standards of decency" and, therefore, the Louisiana statute violated the Eighth Amendment.

Kennedy v. Louisiana
128 S.Ct. 2641 (2008)

Justice Kennedy delivered the opinion of the Court.
Patrick Kennedy, the petitioner here, seeks to set aside his death sentence under the *Eighth Amendment*. He was charged by the respondent, the State of

Sentencing

Louisiana, with the aggravated rape of his then-8-year-old stepdaughter. This case presents the question whether the Constitution bars respondent from imposing the death penalty for the rape of a child where the crime did not result, and was not intended to result, in death of the victim. We hold the *Eighth Amendment* prohibits the death penalty for this offense. The Louisiana statute is unconstitutional.

Petitioner's crime was one that cannot be recounted in these pages in a way sufficient to capture in full the hurt and horror inflicted on his victim or to convey the revulsion society, and the jury that represents it, sought to express by sentencing petitioner to death. [The Court then described the horrific rape of the child. Kennedy was convicted of aggravated rape of the child and sentenced to death.]

The *Eighth Amendment,* applicable to the States through the *Fourteenth Amendment,* provides that "[e]xcessive bail shall not be required, nor excessive fines imposed, nor cruel and unusual punishments inflicted." The Court explained in *Atkins* (2002) and *Roper* (2005) that the *Eighth Amendment's* protection against excessive or cruel and unusual punishments flows from the basic "precept of justice that punishment for [a] crime should be graduated and proportioned to [the] offense." Whether this requirement has been fulfilled is determined not by the standards that prevailed when the *Eighth Amendment* was adopted in 1791 but by the norms that "currently prevail." The Amendment "draw[s] its meaning from the evolving standards of decency that mark the progress of a maturing society." This is because "[t]he standard of extreme cruelty is not merely descriptive, but necessarily embodies a moral judgment. The standard itself remains the same, but its applicability must change as the basic mores of society change."

Applying this principle, we held in *Roper* and *Atkins* that the execution of juveniles and mentally retarded persons are punishments violative of the *Eighth Amendment* because the offender had a diminished personal responsibility for the crime. In these cases the Court has been guided by "objective indicia of society's standards, as expressed in legislative enactments and state practice with respect to executions." Based both on consensus and our own independent judgment, our holding is that a death sentence for one who raped but did not kill a child, and who did not intend to assist another in killing the child, is unconstitutional under the *Eighth* and *Fourteenth Amendments.*

The existence of objective indicia of consensus against making a crime punishable by death was a relevant concern in *Roper, Atkins, Coker,* and *Enmund,* and we follow the approach of those cases here. The history of the death penalty for the crime of rape is an instructive beginning point.

In 1925, 18 States, the District of Columbia, and the Federal Government had statutes that authorized the death penalty for the rape of a child or an adult. See *Coker* (1977) (plurality opinion). Between 1930 and 1964, 455 people were executed for those crimes. To our knowledge the last individual executed for the rape of a child was Ronald Wolfe in 1964.

In 1972, *Furman* invalidated most of the state statutes authorizing the death penalty for the crime of rape; and in *Furman*'s aftermath only six States reenacted their capital rape provisions. Three States—Georgia, North Carolina, and Louisiana—did so with respect to all rape offenses. Three States—Florida, Mississippi, and Tennessee—did so with respect only to child rape.

Louisiana reintroduced the death penalty for rape of a child in 1995. Five States have since followed Louisiana's lead: Georgia, Montana, Oklahoma, South Carolina, and Texas. By contrast, 44 States have not made child rape a capital offense. As for federal law, Congress in the Federal Death Penalty Act of 1994 expanded the number of federal crimes for which the death penalty is a permissible sentence, including certain nonhomicide offenses; but it did not do the same for child rape or abuse.

The evidence of a national consensus with respect to the death penalty for child rapists, as with respect to juveniles, mentally retarded offenders, and vicarious felony murderers, shows divided opinion but, on balance, an opinion against it.

Respondent insists that the six States where child rape is a capital offense, along with the States that have proposed but not yet enacted applicable death penalty legislation, reflect a consistent direction of change in support of the death penalty for child rape. Aside from pending legislation, it is true that in the last 13 years there has been change towards making child rape a capital offense. This is evidenced by six new death penalty statutes, three enacted in the last two years. But this showing is not [significant].

Louisiana is the only State since 1964 that has sentenced an individual to death for the crime of child rape; and petitioner and Richard Davis, who was convicted and sentenced to death for the aggravated rape of a 5-year-old child by a Louisiana jury in December 2007 are the only two individuals now on death row in the United States for a nonhomicide offense.

Our concern here is limited to crimes against individual persons. We do not address, for example, crimes defining and punishing treason, espionage, terrorism, and drug kingpin activity, which are offenses against the State. As it relates to crimes against individuals, though, the death penalty should not be expanded to instances where the victim's life was not taken.

It is not at all evident that the child rape victim's hurt is lessened when the law permits the death of the perpetrator. Capital cases require a long-term commitment by those who testify for the prosecution, especially when guilt and sentencing determinations are in multiple proceedings.

There are, moreover, serious systemic concerns in prosecuting the crime of child rape that are relevant to the constitutionality of making it a capital offense. The problem of unreliable, induced, and even imagined child testimony means there is a "special risk of wrongful execution" in some child rape cases.

In addition, by in effect making the punishment for child rape and murder equivalent, a State that punishes child rape by death may remove a strong incentive for the rapist not to kill the victim.

The rule of evolving standards of decency with specific marks on the way to full progress and mature judgment means that resort to the penalty must be reserved for the worst of crimes and limited in its instances of application. In most cases justice is not better served by terminating the life of the perpetrator rather than confining him and preserving the possibility that he and the system will find ways to allow him to understand the enormity of his offense. Difficulties in administering the penalty to ensure against its arbitrary and capricious application require adherence to a rule reserving its use, at this stage of evolving standards and in cases of crimes against individuals, for crimes that take the life of the victim.

Justice ALITO, with whom THE CHIEF JUSTICE, Justice SCALIA, and Justice THOMAS join, dissenting.

The Court today holds that the *Eighth Amendment* categorically prohibits the imposition of the death penalty for the crime of raping a child. This is so, according to the Court, no matter how young the child, no matter how many times the child is raped, no matter how many children the perpetrator rapes, no matter how sadistic the crime, no matter how much physical or psychological trauma is inflicted, and no matter how heinous the perpetrator's prior criminal record may be. The Court provides two reasons for this sweeping conclusion: First, the Court claims to have identified "a national consensus" that the death penalty is never acceptable for the rape of a child; second, the Court concludes, based on its "independent judgment," that imposing the death penalty for child rape is inconsistent with "'the evolving standards of decency that mark the progress of a maturing society.'" Because neither of these justifications is sound, I respectfully dissent.

The rape of any victim inflicts great injury, and "[s]ome victims are so grievously injured physically or psychologically that life *is* beyond repair." It has been estimated that as many as 40% of 7- to 13-year-old sexual assault victims are considered "seriously disturbed." The harm that is caused to the victims and to society at large by the worst child rapists is grave. It is the judgment of the Louisiana lawmakers and those in an increasing number of other States that these harms justify the death penalty. The Court provides no cogent explanation why this legislative judgment should be overridden. Conclusory references to "decency," "moderation," "restraint," "full progress," and "moral judgment" are not enough.

3.   Recent Limits on the Scope of the Death Penalty

c.   *Method of Execution (casebook page 883) [DVD]*

As discussed in *Harbison v. Little* (p. 883), defendants have challenged lethal injection as cruel and unusual punishment. The Supreme Court decided

Baze v. Kentucky, holding that the specific protocol in Kentucky, as implemented and based on the record in that case, did not violate the Eighth Amendment. However, the Court left the door open for future challenges.

Baze v. Rees

128 S.Ct. 1520 (2008)

Chief Justice ROBERTS announced the judgment of the Court and delivered an opinion, in which Justice KENNEDY and Justice ALITO join.

Like 35 other States and the Federal Government, Kentucky has chosen to impose capital punishment for certain crimes. As is true with respect to each of these States and the Federal Government, Kentucky has altered its method of execution over time to more humane means of carrying out the sentence. That progress has led to the use of lethal injection by every jurisdiction that imposes the death penalty.

Petitioners in this case — each convicted of double homicide — acknowledge that the lethal injection procedure, if applied as intended, will result in a humane death. They nevertheless contend that the lethal injection protocol is unconstitutional under the *Eighth Amendment's* ban on "cruel and unusual punishments," because of the risk that the protocol's terms might not be properly followed, resulting in significant pain. They propose an alternative protocol, one that they concede has not been adopted by any State and has never been tried.

The trial court held extensive hearings and entered detailed Findings of Fact and Conclusions of Law. It recognized that "[t]here are no methods of legal execution that are satisfactory to those who oppose the death penalty on moral, religious, or societal grounds," but concluded that Kentucky's procedure "complies with the constitutional requirements against cruel and unusual punishment." The State Supreme Court affirmed. We too agree that petitioners have not carried their burden of showing that the risk of pain from maladministration of a concededly humane lethal injection protocol, and the failure to adopt untried and untested alternatives, constitute cruel and unusual punishment.

I

By the middle of the 19th century, "hanging was the 'nearly universal form of execution' in the United States." By 1915, 11 other States had followed suit, motivated by the "well-grounded belief that electrocution is less painful and more humane than hanging."

Electrocution remained the predominant mode of execution for nearly a century, although several methods, including hanging, firing squad, and lethal gas were in use at one time. Following the 9-year hiatus in executions that ended with our decision in *Gregg v. Georgia (1976)*, however, state legislatures began responding to public calls to reexamine electrocution as a means of assuring a humane death. In 1977, legislators in Oklahoma, after consulting with the head of the anesthesiology department at the University of Oklahoma College of Medicine, introduced the first bill proposing lethal injection as the State's method of execution. A total of 36 States have now adopted lethal injection as the exclusive or primary means of implementing the death penalty, making it by far the most prevalent method of execution in the United States. It is also the method used by the Federal Government.

Of these 36 States, at least 30 (including Kentucky) use the same combination of three drugs in their lethal injection protocols. The first drug, sodium thiopental (also known as Pentathol), is a fast-acting barbiturate sedative that induces a deep, comalike unconsciousness when given in the amounts used for lethal injection. The second drug, pancuronium bromide (also known as Pavulon), is a paralytic agent that inhibits all muscular-skeletal movements and, by paralyzing the diaphragm, stops respiration. Potassium chloride, the third drug, interferes with the electrical signals that stimulate the contractions of the heart, inducing cardiac arrest. The proper administration of the first drug ensures that the prisoner does not experience any pain associated with the paralysis and cardiac arrest caused by the second and third drugs.

Kentucky replaced electrocution with lethal injection in 1998. The Kentucky statute does not specify the drugs or categories of drugs to be used during an execution, instead mandating that "every death sentence shall be executed by continuous intravenous injection of a substance or combination of substances sufficient to cause death."

Shortly after the adoption of lethal injection, officials working for the Kentucky Department of Corrections set about developing a written protocol for execution. Kentucky's protocol called for the injection of 2 grams of sodium thiopental, 50 milligrams of pancuronium bromide, and 240 milliequivalents of potassium chloride. In 2004, as a result of this litigation, the department chose to increase the amount of sodium thiopental from 2 grams to 3 grams. Between injections, members of the execution team flush the intravenous (IV) lines with 25 milligrams of saline to prevent clogging of the lines by precipitates that may form when residual sodium thiopental comes into contact with pancuronium bromide. The protocol reserves responsibility for inserting the IV catheters to qualified personnel having at least one year of professional experience. Currently, Kentucky uses a certified phlebotomist and an emergency medical technician (EMT) to perform the venipunctures necessary for the catheters. They have up to one hour to establish both primary and secondary peripheral intravenous sites in the arm, hand, leg, or foot of the inmate. Other personnel are responsible for mixing the solutions containing the three drugs and loading them into syringes.

Kentucky's execution facilities consist of the execution chamber, a control room separated by a one-way window, and a witness room. The warden and deputy warden remain in the execution chamber with the prisoner, who is strapped to a gurney. The execution team administers the drugs remotely from the control room through five feet of IV tubing. If, as determined by the warden and deputy warden through visual inspection, the prisoner is not unconscious within 60 seconds following the delivery of the sodium thiopental to the primary IV site, a new 3-gram dose of thiopental is administered to the secondary site before injecting the pancuronium and potassium chloride. In addition to assuring that the first dose of thiopental is successfully administered, the warden and deputy warden also watch for any problems with the IV catheters and tubing.

A physician is present to assist in any effort to revive the prisoner in the event of a last-minute stay of execution. By statute, however, the physician is prohibited from participating in the "conduct of an execution," except to certify the cause of death. An electrocardiogram (EKG) verifies the death of the prisoner. Only one Kentucky prisoner, Eddie Lee Harper, has been executed since the Commonwealth adopted lethal injection. There were no reported problems at Harper's execution.

Petitioners Ralph Baze and Thomas C. Bowling were each convicted of two counts of capital murder and sentenced to death. After a 7-day bench trial during which the trial court received the testimony of approximately 20 witnesses, including numerous experts, the court upheld the protocol, finding there to be minimal risk of various claims of improper administration of the protocol. On appeal, the Kentucky Supreme Court stated that a method of execution violates the *Eighth Amendment* when it "creates a substantial risk of wanton and unnecessary infliction of pain, torture or lingering death."

II

The *Eighth Amendment to the Constitution*, applicable to the States through the *Due Process Clause of the Fourteenth Amendment*, provides that "[e]xcessive bail shall not be required, nor excessive fines imposed, nor cruel and unusual punishments inflicted." We begin with the principle, settled by *Gregg*, that capital punishment is constitutional. It necessarily follows that there must be a means of carrying it out. Some risk of pain is inherent in any method of execution—no matter how humane—if only from the prospect of error in following the required procedure. It is clear, then, that the Constitution does not demand the avoidance of all risk of pain in carrying out executions.

Petitioners do not claim that it does. Rather, they contend that the *Eighth Amendment* prohibits procedures that create an "unnecessary risk" of pain.

Kentucky responds that this "unnecessary risk" standard is tantamount to a requirement that States adopt the " 'least risk' " alternative in carrying out an execution, a standard the Commonwealth contends will cast recurring constitutional doubt on any procedure adopted by the States. Instead, Kentucky urges the Court to approve the " 'substantial risk' " test used by the courts below.

A

This Court has never invalidated a State's chosen procedure for carrying out a sentence of death as the infliction of cruel and unusual punishment.

In *Wilkerson v. Utah* (1879), we upheld a sentence to death by firing squad imposed by a territorial court, rejecting the argument that such a sentence constituted cruel and unusual punishment. We noted there the difficulty of "defin[ing] with exactness the extent of the constitutional provision which provides that cruel and unusual punishments shall not be inflicted." Rather than undertake such an effort, the *Wilkerson* Court simply noted that "it is safe to affirm that punishments of torture, . . . and all others in the same line of unnecessary cruelty, are forbidden" by the *Eighth Amendment*. By way of example, the Court cited cases from England in which "terror, pain, or disgrace were sometimes superadded" to the sentence, such as where the condemned was "embowelled alive, beheaded, and quartered," or instances of "public dissection in murder, and burning alive." In contrast, we observed that the firing squad was routinely used as a method of execution for military officers. What each of the forbidden punishments had in common was the deliberate infliction of pain for the sake of pain— "superadd[ing]" pain to the death sentence through torture and the like.

[W]e observed that "[p]unishments are cruel when they involve torture or a lingering death; but the punishment of death is not cruel within the meaning of that word as used in the Constitution. It implies there something inhuman and barbarous, something more than the mere extinguishment of life."

B

Petitioners do not claim that lethal injection or the proper administration of the particular protocol adopted by Kentucky by themselves constitute the cruel or wanton infliction of pain. Quite the contrary, they concede that "if performed properly," an execution carried out under Kentucky's procedures would be "humane and constitutional."

Instead, petitioners claim that there is a significant risk that the procedures will *not* be properly followed—in particular, that the sodium thiopental will not be properly administered to achieve its intended effect—resulting in severe pain when the other chemicals are administered. Our cases recognize that subjecting individuals to a risk of future harm—not simply actually inflicting pain—can qualify as cruel and unusual punishment. To establish that such exposure violates the *Eighth Amendment*, however, the conditions presenting the risk must be "*sure or very likely* to cause serious illness and needless suffering," and give rise to "sufficiently *imminent* dangers." We have explained that to prevail on such a claim there must be a "substantial risk of serious harm," an "objectively intolerable risk of harm" that prevents prison officials from pleading that they were "subjectively blameless for purposes of the *Eighth Amendment*."

Simply because an execution method may result in pain, either by accident or as an inescapable consequence of death, does not establish the sort of "objectively intolerable risk of harm" that qualifies as cruel and unusual. In *Louisiana ex rel. Francis v. Reswebe* (1947), a plurality of the Court upheld a second attempt at executing a prisoner by electrocution after a mechanical malfunction had interfered with the first attempt. The principal opinion noted that "[a]ccidents happen for which no man is to blame," and concluded that such "an accident, with no suggestion of malevolence."

C

Much of petitioners' case rests on the contention that they have identified a significant risk of harm that can be eliminated by adopting alternative procedures, such as a one-drug protocol that dispenses with the use of pancuronium and potassium chloride, and additional monitoring by trained personnel to ensure that the first dose of sodium thiopental has been adequately delivered. Given what our cases have said about the nature of the risk of harm that is actionable under the *Eighth Amendment,* a condemned prisoner cannot successfully challenge a State's method of execution merely by showing a slightly or marginally safer alternative.

Permitting an *Eighth Amendment* violation to be established on such a showing would threaten to transform courts into boards of inquiry charged with determining "best practices" for executions, with each ruling supplanted by another round of litigation touting a new and improved methodology. Such an approach finds no support in our cases, would embroil the courts in ongoing scientific controversies beyond their expertise, and would substantially intrude on the role of state legislatures in implementing their execution procedures—a role that by all accounts the States have fulfilled with an earnest desire to provide for a progressively more humane manner of death. Accordingly, we reject petitioners' proposed "unnecessary risk" standard, as well as the dissent's "untoward" risk variation.

Instead, the proffered alternatives must effectively address a "substantial risk of serious harm." To qualify, the alternative procedure must be feasible, readily implemented, and in fact significantly reduce a substantial risk of severe pain. If a State refuses to adopt such an alternative in the face of these documented advantages, without a legitimate penological justification for adhering to its current method of execution, then a State's refusal to change its method can be viewed as "cruel and unusual" under the *Eighth Amendment.*[3]

III

In applying these standards to the facts of this case, we note at the outset that it is difficult to regard a practice as "objectively intolerable" when it is in fact widely tolerated. Thirty-six States that sanction capital punishment have adopted lethal injection as the preferred method of execution. The Federal Government uses lethal injection as well. This broad consensus goes not just to the method of execution, but also to the specific three-drug combination used by Kentucky. Thirty States, as well as the Federal Government, use a series of sodium thiopental, pancuronium bromide, and potassium chloride, in varying amounts. No State uses or has ever used the alternative one-drug protocol belatedly urged by petitioners.

We agree with the state trial court and State Supreme Court that petitioners have not shown that the risk of an inadequate dose of the first drug is substantial. And we reject the argument that the *Eighth Amendment* requires Kentucky to adopt the untested alternative procedures petitioners have identified.

Reasonable people of good faith disagree on the morality and efficacy of capital punishment, and for many who oppose it, no method of execution would ever be acceptable. But as Justice Frankfurter stressed in *Resweber*, "[o]ne must be on guard against finding in personal disapproval a reflection of more or less prevailing condemnation." This Court has ruled that capital punishment is not prohibited under our Constitution, and that the States may enact laws specifying that sanction.

Kentucky has adopted a method of execution believed to be the most humane available, one it shares with 35 other States. Petitioners agree that, if administered as intended, that procedure will result in a painless death. The risks of maladministration they have suggested—such as improper mixing of chemicals and improper setting of IVs by trained and experienced personnel—cannot remotely be characterized as "objectively intolerable." Kentucky's decision to adhere to its protocol despite these asserted risks, while adopting safeguards to protect against them, cannot be viewed as probative of the wanton infliction of pain under the *Eighth Amendment*. Finally, the alternative that petitioners belatedly propose has problems of its own, and has never been tried by a single State.

The broad framework of the *Eighth Amendment* has accommodated . . . progress toward more humane methods of execution, and our approval of a particular method in the past has not precluded legislatures from taking the steps they deem appropriate, in light of new developments, to ensure humane capital punishment. There is no reason to suppose that today's decision will be any different.

The judgment below concluding that Kentucky's procedure is consistent with the *Eighth Amendment* is, accordingly, affirmed.

Justice ALITO, concurring.

I join the plurality opinion but write separately to explain my view of how the holding should be implemented.

Prominent among the practical constraints that must be taken into account in considering the feasibility and availability of any suggested modification of a lethal injection protocol are the ethical restrictions applicable to medical professionals. The first step in the lethal injection protocols currently in use is the anesthetization of the prisoner. If this step is carried out properly, it is agreed, the prisoner will not experience pain during the remainder of the procedure. Every day, general anesthetics are administered to surgical patients in this country, and if the medical professionals who participate in these surgeries also participated in the anesthetization of prisoners facing execution by lethal injection, the risk of pain would be minimized. But the ethics rules of medical professionals—for reasons that I certainly do not question here—prohibit their participation in executions.

Objections to features of a lethal injection protocol must be considered against the backdrop of the ethics rules of medical professionals and related practical constraints. Assuming, as previously discussed, that lethal injection is not unconstitutional *per se*, it follows that a suggested modification of a lethal injection protocol cannot be regarded as "feasible" or "readily" available if the modification would require participation—either in carrying out the execution or in training those who carry out the execution—by persons whose professional ethics rules or traditions impede their participation.

The issue presented in this case—the constitutionality of a *method* of execution—should be kept separate from the controversial issue of the death penalty itself. If the Court wishes to reexamine the latter issue, it should do so directly, as Justice Stevens now suggests. The Court should not produce a *de facto* ban on capital punishment by adopting method-of-execution rules that lead to litigation gridlock.

Justice STEVENS, concurring in the judgment.

When we granted certiorari in this case, I assumed that our decision would bring the debate about lethal injection as a method of execution to a close. It now seems clear that it will not. The question whether a similar three-drug protocol may be used in other States remains open, and may well be answered differently in a future case on the basis of a more complete record. Instead of ending the controversy, I am now convinced that this case will generate debate not only about the constitutionality of the three-drug protocol, and specifically about the justification for the use of the paralytic agent, pancuronium bromide, but also about the justification for the death penalty itself.

I

Because it masks any outward sign of distress, pancuronium bromide creates a risk that the inmate will suffer excruciating pain before death occurs. There is a general understanding among veterinarians that the risk of pain is sufficiently serious that the use of the drug should be proscribed when an animal's life is being terminated. As a result of this understanding among knowledgeable professionals, several States—including Kentucky—have enacted legislation prohibiting use of the drug in animal euthanasia. It is unseemly—to say the least—that Kentucky may well kill petitioners using a drug that it would not permit to be used on their pets.

Use of pancuronium bromide is particularly disturbing because—as the trial court specifically found in this case—it serves "no therapeutic purpose." The drug's primary use is to prevent involuntary muscle movements, and its secondary use is to stop respiration. In my view, neither of these purposes is sufficient to justify the risk inherent in the use of the drug.

The plurality believes that preventing involuntary movement is a legitimate justification for using pancuronium bromide because "[t]he Commonwealth has an interest in preserving the dignity of the procedure, especially where convulsions or seizures could be misperceived as signs of consciousness or distress." This is a woefully inadequate justification. Whatever minimal interest there may be in ensuring that a condemned inmate dies a dignified death, and that witnesses to the execution are not made uncomfortable by an incorrect belief (which could easily be corrected) that the inmate is in pain, is vastly outweighed by the risk that the inmate is actually experiencing excruciating pain that no one can detect.[3]

In my view, therefore, States wishing to decrease the risk that future litigation will delay executions or invalidate their protocols would do well to reconsider their continued use of pancuronium bromide.

II

The thoughtful opinions written by THE CHIEF JUSTICE and by JUSTICE GINSBURG have persuaded me that current decisions by state legislatures, by the Congress of the United States, and by this Court to retain the death penalty as a part of our law are the product of habit and inattention rather than an acceptable deliberative process that weighs the costs and risks of administering that penalty against its identifiable benefits, and rest in part on a faulty assumption about the retributive force of the death penalty.

In *Gregg v. Georgia (1976)*, we explained that unless a criminal sanction serves a legitimate penological function, it constitutes "gratuitous infliction of suffering" in violation of the *Eighth Amendment*. We then identified three societal purposes for death as a sanction: incapacitation, deterrence, and retribution. In the past three decades, however, each of these rationales has been called into question.

While incapacitation may have been a legitimate rationale in 1976, the recent rise in statutes providing for life imprisonment without the possibility of parole demonstrates that incapacitation is neither a necessary nor a sufficient justification for the death penalty. Moreover, a recent poll indicates that support for the death penalty drops significantly when life without the possibility of parole is presented as an alternative option. And the available sociological evidence suggests that juries are less likely to impose the death penalty when life without parole is available as a sentence.

The legitimacy of deterrence as an acceptable justification for the death penalty is also questionable, at best. Despite 30 years of empirical research in the area, there remains no reliable statistical evidence that capital punishment in fact deters potential offenders. In the absence of such evidence, deterrence cannot serve as a sufficient penological justification for this uniquely severe and irrevocable punishment.

We are left, then, with retribution as the primary rationale for imposing the death penalty. And indeed, it is the retribution rationale that animates much of the remaining enthusiasm for the death penalty. At the same time, . . . our society has moved away from public and painful retribution towards ever more humane forms of punishment. State-sanctioned killing is therefore becoming more and more anachronistic. In an attempt to bring executions in line with our evolving standards of decency, we have adopted increasingly less painful methods of execution, and then declared previous methods barbaric and archaic. But by requiring that an execution be relatively painless, we necessarily protect the inmate from enduring any punishment that is comparable to the suffering inflicted on his victim. This trend, while appropriate and required by the *Eighth Amendment's* prohibition on cruel and unusual punishment, actually undermines the very premise on which public approval of the retribution rationale is based.[1]

Full recognition of the diminishing force of the principal rationales for retaining the death penalty should lead this Court and legislatures to reexamine the question recently posed by Professor Salinas, a former Texas prosecutor and judge: "The time for a dispassionate, impartial comparison of the enormous costs that death penalty litigation imposes on society with the benefits that it produces has surely arrived.

III

Our decisions in 1976 upholding the constitutionality of the death penalty relied heavily on our belief that adequate procedures were in place that would avoid the danger of discriminatory application identified by Justice Douglas' opinion in *Furman*. Ironically, however, more recent cases have endorsed procedures that provide less protections to capital defendants than to ordinary offenders. Of special concern to me are rules that deprive the defendant of a trial by jurors representing a fair cross section of the community. Litigation involving both challenges for cause and peremptory challenges has persuaded me that the process of obtaining a "death qualified jury" is really a procedure that has the purpose and effect of obtaining a jury that is biased in favor of conviction.

Another serious concern is that the risk of error in capital cases may be greater than in other cases because the facts are often so disturbing that the interest in making sure the crime does not go unpunished may overcome residual doubt concerning the identity of the offender.

A third significant concern is the risk of discriminatory application of the death penalty. While that risk has been dramatically reduced, the Court has allowed it to continue to play an unacceptable role in capital cases.

Finally, given the real risk of error in this class of cases, the irrevocable nature of the consequences is of decisive importance to me. Whether or not any innocent defendants have actually been executed, abundant evidence accumulated in recent years has resulted in the exoneration of an unacceptable number of defendants found guilty of capital offenses. The risk of executing innocent defendants can be entirely eliminated by treating any penalty more severe than life imprisonment without the possibility of parole as constitutionally excessive.

---

1. For example, one survivor of the Oklahoma City bombing expressed a belief that " 'death by [lethal] injection [was] "too good" for McVeigh.' "

In sum, . . . I have relied on my own experience in reaching the conclusion that the imposition of the death penalty represents "the pointless and needless extinction of life with only marginal contributions to any discernible social or public purposes. A penalty with such negligible returns to the State [is] patently excessive and cruel and unusual punishment violative of the *Eighth Amendment.*"

IV

The conclusion that I have reached with regard to the constitutionality of the death penalty itself makes my decision in this case particularly difficult. It does not, however, justify a refusal to respect precedents that remain a part of our law. This Court has held that the death penalty is constitutional, and has established a framework for evaluating the constitutionality of particular methods of execution. Under those precedents, . . . I am persuaded that the evidence adduced by petitioners fails to prove that Kentucky's lethal injection protocol violates the *Eighth Amendment.* Accordingly, I join the Court's judgment.

Justice SCALIA, with whom Justice THOMAS joins, concurring in the judgment.

I write separately to provide what I think is needed response to Justice STEVENS' separate opinion.

Justice Stevens concludes as follows: "[T]he imposition of the death penalty represents the pointless and needless extinction of life with only marginal contributions to any discernible social or public purposes. A penalty with such negligible returns to the State [is] patently excessive and cruel and unusual punishment violative of the *Eighth Amendment.*"

This conclusion is insupportable as an interpretation of the Constitution, which generally leaves it to democratically elected legislatures rather than courts to decide what makes significant contribution to social or public purposes. Besides that more general proposition, the very text of the document recognizes that the death penalty is a permissible legislative choice.

According to Justice Stevens, the death penalty promotes none of the purposes of criminal punishment because it neither prevents more crimes than alternative measures nor serves a retributive purpose.

These conclusions are not supported by the available data. Justice Stevens' analysis barely acknowledges the "significant body of recent evidence that capital punishment may well have a deterrent effect, possibly a quite powerful one." According to a "leading national study," "each execution prevents some eighteen murders, on average." "If the current evidence is even roughly correct . . . then a refusal to impose capital punishment will effectively condemn numerous innocent people to death."

But even if Justice Stevens' assertion about the deterrent value of the death penalty were correct, the death penalty would yet be constitutional (as he concedes) if it served the appropriate purpose of retribution. "[T]he decision that capital punishment may be the appropriate sanction in extreme cases is an expression of the community's belief that certain crimes are themselves so grievous an affront to humanity that the only adequate response may be the penalty of death.

Justice Stevens' final refuge in his cost-benefit analysis is a familiar one: There is a risk that an innocent person might be convicted and sentenced to death. That rationale, however, supports not Justice Stevens' conclusion that the death penalty is unconstitutional, but the more sweeping proposition that any conviction in a case in which facts are disturbing is suspect—including, of course, convictions resulting in life without parole in those States that do not have capital punishment. The same is true of Justice Stevens' claim that there is a risk of "discriminatory application of the death penalty." The same could be said of any criminal penalty, including life without parole; there is no proof that in this regard the death penalty is distinctive.

But of all Justice Stevens' criticisms of the death penalty, the hardest to take is his bemoaning of "the enormous costs that death penalty litigation imposes on society," including the "burden on the courts and the lack of finality for victim's families." Those costs, those burdens, and that lack of finality are in large measure the creation of Justice Stevens and other Justices opposed to the death penalty, who have "encumber[ed] [it] . . . with unwarranted restrictions neither contained in the text of the Constitution nor reflected in two centuries of practice under it"— the product of their policy views "not shared by the vast majority of the American people."

I take no position on the desirability of the death penalty, except to say that its value is eminently debatable and the subject of deeply, indeed passionately, held views—which means, to me, that it is preeminently not a matter to be resolved here. And especially not when it is explicitly permitted by the Constitution.

Justice THOMAS, with whom Justice SCALIA joins, concurring in the judgment.

Although I agree that petitioners have failed to establish that Kentucky's lethal injection protocol violates the *Eighth Amendment*, I write separately because I cannot subscribe to the plurality opinion's formulation of the governing standard. As I understand it, that opinion would hold that a method of execution violates the *Eighth Amendment* if it poses a substantial risk of severe pain that could be significantly reduced by adopting readily available alternative procedures. This standard—along with petitioners' proposed "unnecessary risk" standard and the dissent's "untoward risk" standard,—finds no support in the original understanding of the *Cruel and Unusual Punishments Clause* or in our previous method-of-execution cases; casts constitutional doubt on long-accepted methods of execution; and injects the Court into matters it has no institutional capacity to resolve. Because, in my view, a method of execution violates the *Eighth Amendment* only if it is deliberately designed to inflict pain, I concur only in the judgment.

In English and early colonial practice, the death penalty was not a uniform punishment, but rather a range of punishments, some of which the Framers likely regarded as cruel and unusual. Death by hanging was the most common mode of execution. "An ordinary death by hanging was not, however, the harshest penalty at the disposal of the seventeenth- and eighteenth-century state." In addition to hanging, which was intended to, and often did, result in a quick and painless death, "[o]fficials also wielded a set of tools capable of *intensifying* a death sentence," that is, "ways of producing a punishment worse than death."

One such "tool" was burning at the stake. Because burning, unlike hanging, was always painful and destroyed the body, it was considered "a form of super-capital punishment, worse than death itself." Reserved for offenders whose crimes were thought to pose an especially grave threat to the social order—such as slaves who killed their masters and women who killed their husbands—burning a person alive was so dreadful a punishment that sheriffs sometimes hanged the offender first "as an act of charity."

Other methods of intensifying a death sentence included "gibbeting," or hanging the condemned in an iron cage so that his body would decompose in public view and "public dissection". But none of these was the worst fate a criminal could meet. That was reserved for the most dangerous and reprobate offenders—traitors. "The punishment of high treason," Blackstone wrote, was "very solemn and terrible," and involved "embowelling alive, beheading, and quartering," Thus, the following death sentence could be pronounced on seven men convicted of high treason in England:

> " 'That you and each of you, be taken to the place from whence you came, and from thence be drawn on a hurdle to the place of execution, where you shall be hanged by the necks, not till you are dead; that you be severally taken down, while yet alive, and your bowels be taken out and burnt before your faces—that your heads be then cut off, and your bodies cut in four quarters, to be at the King's disposal. And God Almighty have mercy on your souls.' "*

The principal object of these aggravated forms of capital punishment was to terrorize the criminal, and thereby more effectively deter the crime. Their defining characteristic was that they were purposely designed to inflict pain and suffering beyond that necessary to cause death. Early commentators on the Constitution likewise interpreted the *Cruel and Unusual Punishments Clause* as referring to torturous punishments.

We have never suggested that a method of execution is "cruel and unusual" within the meaning of the *Eighth Amendment* simply because it involves a risk of pain—whether "substantial," "unnecessary," or "untoward"—that could be reduced by adopting alternative procedures. Quite plainly, what defined ["cruel and unusual"] punishments was that they were *designed* to inflict torture as a way of enhancing a death sentence; they were *intended* to produce a penalty worse than death, to accomplish something "more than the mere extinguishment of life."

I reject as both unprecedented and unworkable any standard that would require the courts to weigh the relative advantages and disadvantages of different methods of execution or of different procedures for implementing a given method of execution.

Judged under the proper standard, this is an easy case. Because Kentucky's lethal injection protocol is designed to eliminate pain rather than to inflict it, petitioners' challenge must fail.

Justice BREYER, concurring in the judgment.

In respect to *how* a court should review such a claim, I agree with Justice GINSBURG. She highlights the relevant question, whether the method creates an untoward, readily avoidable risk of inflicting severe and unnecessary suffering. [However], I cannot find, either in the record in this case or in the literature on the subject, sufficient evidence that Kentucky's execution method poses the "significant and unnecessary risk of inflicting severe pain" that petitioners assert.

Justice GINSBURG, with whom Justice SOUTER joins, dissenting.

The constitutionality of Kentucky's protocol therefore turns on whether inmates are adequately anesthetized by the first drug in the protocol, sodium thiopental. Kentucky's system is constitutional, the plurality states, because "petitioners have not shown that the risk of an inadequate dose of the first drug is substantial." I would not dispose of the case so swiftly given the character of the risk at stake. Kentucky's protocol lacks basic safeguards used by other States to confirm that an inmate is unconscious before injection of the second and third drugs. I would vacate and remand with instructions to consider whether Kentucky's omission of those safeguards poses an untoward, readily avoidable risk of inflicting severe and unnecessary pain.

Chapter 14

DOUBLE JEOPARDY

F. Collateral Estoppel (casebook page 919)

In *Ashe v. Swenson* (1970), the Court established that Double Jeopardy barred retrial of issues that were necessarily decided in a prior case. In *Yeager v. United States* (2009), a slim majority of Justices applied this principle to counts being retried as the result of a mistrial in the first trial.

Yeager v. United States
2009 U.S. LEXIS 4538 (2009)

JUSTICE STEVENS delivered the opinion of the Court.

The question presented in this case is whether an apparent inconsistency between a jury's verdict of acquittal on some counts and its failure to return a verdict on other counts affects the preclusive force of the acquittals under the *Double Jeopardy Clause of the Fifth Amendment.* We hold that it does not.

I

[Petitioner F. Scott Yeager served as an officer for a division of Enron Corporation (Enron). He was in charge of a project there called EIN. At the company's annual conference, Yeager allegedly made false and misleading statements about the value and performance of the EIN project. Thereafter, the price of Enron stock rose from $54 to $67. The next day it reached $72. At that point petitioner sold more than 100,000 shares of Enron stock that he had received as part of his compensation. During the next several months petitioner sold an additional 600,000 shares. All told, petitioner's stock sales generated more than $54 million in proceeds and $19 million in personal profit. As it turned out, the EIN project turned out to be worthless.]

[In 2004], a grand jury returned a "Fifth Superseding Indictment" charging petitioner with 126 counts of five federal offenses: (1)conspiracy to commit securities and wire fraud; (2)securities fraud; (3)wire fraud; (4)insider trading; and (5)money laundering. The Government's theory of prosecution was that petitioner—acting in concert with other Enron executives—purposefully deceived the public about the EIN project in order to inflate the value of Enron's stock and, ultimately, to enrich himself. [Counts 1 through 6 were the "fraud counts" and the remaining counts were "insider trading counts."]

The trial lasted 13 weeks. After four days of deliberations, the jury notified the court that it had reached agreement on some counts but had deadlocked on others. The jury acquitted petitioner on the fraud counts but failed to reach a verdict on the insider trading counts. The court entered judgment on the acquittals and declared a mistrial on the hung counts.

[Thereafter], the Government obtained a new indictment against petitioner. This "Eighth Superseding Indictment" recharged petitioner with some, but not all, of the insider trading counts on which the jury had previously hung. [T]he new indictment focused on petitioner's knowledge of the EIN project and his failure to disclose that information to the public before selling his Enron stock.

Petitioner moved to dismiss all counts in the new indictment on the ground that the acquittals on the fraud counts precluded the Government from retrying him on the insider trading counts. He argued that the jury's acquittals had necessarily decided that he did not possess material, nonpublic information about the performance of the EIN project and its value to Enron. In petitioner's view, because reprosecution for insider trading would require the Government to prove that critical fact, the issue-preclusion component of the *Double Jeopardy Clause* barred a second trial of that issue and mandated dismissal of all of the insider trading counts.

The District Court denied the motion. After reviewing the trial record, the court disagreed with petitioner's reading of what the jury necessarily decided. In the court's telling, the jury likely concluded that petitioner "did not knowingly and willfully participate in the scheme to defraud described in the conspiracy, securities fraud, and wire fraud counts." The court therefore concluded that the question whether petitioner possessed insider information was not necessarily resolved in the first trial and could be litigated anew in a second prosecution.

The Court of Appeals disagreed with the District Court's analysis of the record, but nevertheless affirmed. It reasoned that petitioner "did not dispute" the Government's theory that he "helped shape the message" of the allegedly fraudulent presentations made at the analyst conference, and therefore rejected the District Court's conclusion that the jury had "acquitted [petitioner] on the groun[d] that he did not participate in the fraud." Based on its independent review of the record, the Court of Appeals instead concluded that "the jury must have found when it acquitted [petitioner] that [he] did not have any insider information that contradicted what was presented to the public." The court acknowledged that this factual determination would normally preclude the Government from retrying petitioner for insider trading or money laundering.

The court was nevertheless persuaded that a truly rational jury, having concluded that petitioner did not have any insider information, would have *acquitted* him on the insider trading counts. That the jury failed to acquit, and instead hung on those counts, was pivotal in the court's issue-preclusion analysis. Considering "the hung counts along with the acquittals," the court found it impossible "to decide with any certainty what the jury necessarily determined."

Several courts have taken the contrary view and have held that a jury's failure to reach a verdict on some counts should play no role in determining the preclusive effect of an acquittal. Others have sided with the Court of Appeals. We granted certiorari to resolve the conflict and now reverse.

II

The *Double Jeopardy Clause of the Fifth Amendment* provides: "[N]or shall any person be subject for the same offence to be twice put in jeopardy of life or limb."

Our cases have recognized that the Clause embodies two vitally important interests. The first is the "deeply ingrained" principle that "the State with all its resources and power should not be allowed to make repeated attempts to convict an individual for an alleged offense, thereby subjecting him to embarrassment, expense and ordeal and compelling him to live in a continuing state of anxiety and insecurity, as well as enhancing the possibility that even though innocent he may be found guilty." The second interest is the preservation of "the finality of judgments."

The first interest is implicated whenever the State seeks a second trial after its first attempt to obtain a conviction results in a mistrial because the jury has failed to reach a verdict. In these circumstances, however, while the defendant has an interest in avoiding multiple trials, the Clause does not prevent the Government from seeking to reprosecute. Despite the argument's textual appeal, we have held that the second trial does not place the defendant in jeopardy "twice."

While the case before us involves a mistrial on the insider trading counts, the question presented cannot be resolved by asking whether the Government should be given one complete opportunity to convict petitioner on those charges. Rather, the case turns on the second interest at the core of the Clause. We must determine whether the interest in preserving the finality of the jury's judgment on the fraud counts, including the jury's finding that petitioner did not possess insider information, bars a retrial on the insider trading counts. The proper question, under the Clause's text, is whether it is appropriate to treat the insider trading charges as the "same offence" as the fraud charges. Our opinion in *Ashe v. Swenson* (1970), provides the basis for our answer.

In *Ashe*, we squarely held that the *Double Jeopardy Clause* precludes the Government from relitigating any issue that was necessarily decided by a jury's acquittal in a prior trial. In that case, six poker players were robbed by a group of masked men. Ashe was charged with — and acquitted of — robbing Donald Knight, one of the six players. The State sought to retry Ashe for the robbery of another poker player only weeks after the first jury had acquitted him. The second prosecution was successful: Facing "substantially stronger" testimony from "witnesses [who] were for the most part the same," Ashe was convicted and sentenced to a 35-year prison term. We concluded that the subsequent prosecution was constitutionally prohibited. Because the only contested issue at the first trial was whether Ashe was one of the robbers, we held that the jury's verdict of acquittal collaterally estopped the State from trying him for robbing a different player during the same criminal episode. We explained that "when an issue of ultimate fact has once been determined by a valid and final judgment" of acquittal, it "cannot again be litigated" in a second trial for a separate offense. To decipher what a jury has necessarily decided, we held that courts should "examine the record of a prior proceeding, taking into account the pleadings, evidence, charge, and other relevant matter, and conclude whether a rational jury could have grounded its verdict upon an issue other than that which the defendant seeks to foreclose from consideration."

[T]he Court of Appeals reasoned that the hung counts must be considered to determine what issues the jury decided in the first trial. Viewed in isolation, the court explained, the acquittals on the fraud charges would preclude retrial because they appeared to support petitioner's argument that the jury decided he lacked insider information. Viewed alongside the hung counts, however, the acquittals appeared less decisive. The problem, as the court saw it, was that, if "the jury found that [petitioner] did not have insider information, then the jury, acting rationally, would also have acquitted [him] of the insider trading counts." The fact that the jury hung was a logical wrinkle that made it impossible for the court "to decide with any certainty what the jury necessarily determined." Because petitioner failed to show what the jury decided, the court refused to find the Government precluded from pursuing the hung counts in a new prosecution.

The Court of Appeals' issue-preclusion analysis was in error. A hung count is not a "relevant" part of the "record of [the] prior proceeding." Because a jury speaks only through its verdict, its failure to reach a verdict cannot — by negative implication — yield a piece of information that helps put together the trial puzzle. A mistried count is therefore nothing like the other forms of record material that *Ashe* suggested should be part of the preclusion inquiry. A host of reasons — sharp disagreement, confusion about the issues, exhaustion after a long trial, to name but a few — could work alone or in tandem to cause a jury to hang. To ascribe meaning to a hung count would presume an ability to identify which factor was at play in the jury room. But that is not reasoned analysis; it is guesswork. Such conjecture about possible reasons for a jury's failure to reach a decision should play no part in assessing the legal consequences of a unanimous verdict that the jurors did return.

To identify what a jury necessarily determined at trial, courts should scrutinize a jury's decisions, not its failures to decide. Thus, if the possession of insider information was a critical issue of ultimate fact in all of the charges against petitioner, a jury verdict that necessarily decided that issue in his favor protects him from prosecution for any charge for which that is an essential element.

IV

[W]e decline to engage in a fact-intensive analysis of the voluminous record [to determine the basis for the acquittal]. If it chooses, the Court of Appeals may revisit its factual analysis in light of the Government's arguments before this Court.

Double Jeopardy

Justice KENNEDY, concurring in part and concurring in the judgment.

It is insufficient for the Court to say that, on remand, the Court of Appeals "may," "[i]f it chooses," "revisit its factual analysis." The correct course would be to require the Court of Appeals to do so.

Justice SCALIA, with whom Justice THOMAS and Justice ALITO join, dissenting.

Ashe held only that the Clause sometimes bars successive prosecution of facts found during "a prior proceeding." But today the Court bars retrial on hung counts after what was not, under this Court's theory of "continuing jeopardy," a prior proceeding but simply an earlier stage of the same proceeding.

Today's holding interprets the *Double Jeopardy Clause*, for the first time, to have effect internally within a single prosecution, even though the "'criminal proceedings against [the] accused have not run their full course.'"

The burdens created by the Court's opinion today are likely to be substantial. The *Ashe* inquiry will require courts to "examine the record of a prior proceeding, taking into account the pleadings, evidence, charge, and other relevant matter, and conclude whether a rational jury could have grounded its verdict upon an issue other than that which the defendant seeks to foreclose from consideration." What is more, our holding in *Abney v. United States*, 51 (1977), ensures that every defendant in Yeager's shoes will be entitled to an immediate interlocutory appeal (and petition for certiorari) whenever his *Ashe* claim is rejected by the trial court.

Until today, this Court has consistently held that retrial after a jury has been unable to reach a verdict is part of the original prosecution and that there can be no second jeopardy where there has been no second prosecution. I would affirm the judgment.

Chapter 15

HABEAS CORPUS

D.   Habeas Corpus and the War on Terrorism
   (insert page 1017)

In June 2008, in *Boumediene v. Bush*, the Supreme Court considered whether the Detainee Treatment Act and the Military Commission Act are unconstitutional in limiting access to habeas corpus by non-citizens held as enemy combatants. The decision focuses on what the Constitution requires in terms of the availability of habeas corpus; specifically, what is an unconstitutional suspension of the writ? Underlying the majority and the dissenting are very different views about the appropriate role of the judiciary in the war on terror.

Boumediene v. Bush
128 S.Ct. 2229 (2008)

Justice KENNEDY delivered the opinion of the Court.

Petitioners are aliens designated as enemy combatants and detained at the United States Naval Station at Guantanamo Bay, Cuba. There are others detained there, also aliens, who are not parties to this suit.

Petitioners present a question not resolved by our earlier cases relating to the detention of aliens at Guantanamo: whether they have the constitutional privilege of habeas corpus, a privilege not to be withdrawn except in conformance with the Suspension Clause, Art. I, §9, cl. 2. We hold these petitioners do have the habeas corpus privilege. Congress has enacted a statute, the Detainee Treatment Act of 2005(DTA), that provides certain procedures for review of the detainees' status. We hold that those procedures are not an adequate and effective substitute for habeas corpus. Therefore §7 of the Military Commissions Act of 2006(MCA), operates as an unconstitutional suspension of the writ. We do not address whether the President has authority to detain these petitioners nor do we hold that the writ must issue. These and other questions regarding the legality of the detention are to be resolved in the first instance by the District Court.

I

Under the Authorization for Use of Military Force (AUMF), the President is authorized "to use all necessary and appropriate force against those nations, organizations, or persons he determines planned, authorized, committed, or aided the terrorist attacks that occurred on September 11, 2001, or harbored such organizations or persons, in order to prevent any future acts of international terrorism against the United States by such nations, organizations or persons."

In Hamdi v. Rumsfeld (2004), five Members of the Court recognized that detention of individuals who fought against the United States in Afghanistan "for the duration of the particular conflict in which they were captured, is so fundamental and accepted an incident to war as to be an exercise of the 'necessary and appropriate force' Congress has authorized the President to use." After Hamdi, the Deputy Secretary of Defense established Combatant Status Review Tribunals (CSRTs) to determine whether individuals detained at Guantanamo were "enemy combatants," as the Department defines that term. A later memorandum established procedures to implement the CSRTs. The Government maintains these procedures were designed to comply with the due process requirements identified by the plurality in Hamdi.

Interpreting the AUMF, the Department of Defense ordered the detention of these petitioners, and they were transferred to Guantanamo. Some of these individuals were apprehended on the battlefield in Afghanistan, others in places as far away from there as Bosnia and Gambia. All are foreign nationals, but none is a citizen of a nation now at war with the United States. Each denies he is a member of the al Qaeda terrorist network that carried out the September 11 attacks or of the Taliban regime that provided sanctuary for al Qaeda. Each petitioner appeared before a separate CSRT; was determined to be an enemy combatant; and has sought a writ of habeas corpus in the United States District Court for the District of Columbia.

The first actions commenced in February 2002. We granted certiorari and reversed, holding that 28 U.S.C. §2241 extended statutory habeas corpus jurisdiction to Guantanamo. See Rasul v. Bush (2004). After Rasul, petitioners' cases were consolidated and entertained in two separate proceedings. In the first set of cases, Judge Richard J. Leon granted the Government's motion to dismiss, holding that the detainees had no rights that could be vindicated in a habeas corpus action. In the second set of cases Judge Joyce Hens Green reached the opposite conclusion, holding the detainees had rights under the Due Process Clause of the Fifth Amendment.

While appeals were pending from the District Court decisions, Congress passed the DTA. Subsection (e) of §1005 of the DTA amended 28 U.S.C. §2241 to provide that "no court, justice, or judge shall have jurisdiction to hear or consider . . . an application for a writ of habeas corpus filed by or on behalf of an alien detained by the Department of Defense at Guantanamo Bay, Cuba." Section 1005 further provides that the Court of Appeals for the District of Columbia Circuit shall have "exclusive" jurisdiction to review decisions of the CSRTs. Ibid.

In Hamdan v. Rumsfeld (2006), the Court held this provision did not apply to cases (like petitioners') pending when the DTA was enacted. Congress responded by passing the MCA.

II

As a threshold matter, we must decide whether MCA §7 denies the federal courts jurisdiction to hear habeas corpus actions pending at the time of its enactment. We hold the statute does deny that jurisdiction, so that, if the statute is valid, petitioners' cases must be dismissed.

As amended by the terms of the MCA, 28 U.S.C.A. §2241(e) now provides:

"(1) No court, justice, or judge shall have jurisdiction to hear or consider an application for a writ of habeas corpus filed by or on behalf of an alien detained by the United States who has been determined by the United States to have been properly detained as an enemy combatant or is awaiting such determination.

"(2) Except as provided in [§§1005(e)(2) and (e)(3) of the DTA] no court, justice, or judge shall have jurisdiction to hear or consider any other action against the United States or its agents relating to any aspect of the detention, transfer, treatment, trial, or conditions of confinement of an alien who is or was detained by the United States and has been determined by the United States to have been properly detained as an enemy combatant or is awaiting such determination."

Section 7(b) of the MCA provides the effective date for the amendment of §2241(e). It states: "The amendment made by [MCA §7(a)] shall take effect on the date of the enactment of this Act, and shall apply to all cases, without exception, pending on or after the date of the enactment of this Act which relate to any aspect of the detention, transfer, treatment, trial, or conditions of detention of an alien detained by the United States since September 11, 2001."

If this ongoing dialogue between and among the branches of Government is to be respected, we cannot ignore that the MCA was a direct response to Hamdan's holding that the DTA's jurisdiction-stripping provision had no application to pending cases. The Court of Appeals was correct to take note of the legislative history when construing the statute, and we agree with its conclusion that the MCA deprives the federal courts of jurisdiction to entertain the habeas corpus actions now before us.

III

In deciding the constitutional questions now presented we must determine whether petitioners are barred from seeking the writ or invoking the protections of the Suspension Clause either because of their status, i.e., petitioners' designation by the Executive Branch as enemy combatants, or their physical location, i.e., their presence at Guantanamo Bay. The Government contends that noncitizens designated as enemy combatants and detained in territory located outside our Nation's borders have no constitutional rights and no privilege of habeas corpus. Petitioners contend they do have cognizable constitutional rights and that Congress, in seeking to eliminate recourse to habeas corpus as a means to assert those rights, acted in violation of the Suspension Clause.

A

The Framers viewed freedom from unlawful restraint as a fundamental precept of liberty, and they understood the writ of habeas corpus as a vital instrument to secure that freedom. Experience taught, however, that the common-law writ all too often had been insufficient to guard against the abuse of monarchial power. That history counseled the necessity for specific language in the Constitution to secure the writ and ensure its place in our legal system.

That the Framers considered the writ a vital instrument for the protection of individual liberty is evident from the care taken to specify the limited grounds for its suspension: "The Privilege of the Writ of Habeas Corpus shall not be suspended, unless when in Cases of Rebellion or Invasion the public Safety may require it." Art. I, §9, cl. 2. The word "privilege" was used, perhaps, to avoid mentioning some rights to the exclusion of others. (Indeed, the only mention of the term "right" in the Constitution, as ratified, is in its clause giving Congress the power to protect the rights of authors and inventors. See Art. I, §8, cl. 8.) Surviving accounts of the ratification debates provide additional evidence that the Framers deemed the writ to be an essential mechanism in the separation-of-powers scheme.

In our own system the Suspension Clause is designed to protect against these cyclical abuses. The Clause protects the rights of the detained by a means consistent with the essential design of the Constitution. It ensures that, except during periods of formal suspension, the Judiciary will have a time-tested device, the writ, to maintain the "delicate balance of governance" that is itself the surest safeguard of liberty. The Clause protects the rights of the detained by affirming the duty and authority of the Judiciary to call the jailer to account.

B

The broad historical narrative of the writ and its function is central to our analysis, but we seek guidance as well from founding-era authorities addressing the specific question before us: whether foreign nationals, apprehended and detained in distant countries during a time of serious threats to our Nation's security, may assert the privilege of the writ and seek its protection. The Court has been careful not to foreclose the possibility that the protections of the Suspension Clause have expanded along with post-1789 developments that define the present scope of the writ. But the analysis may begin with precedents as of 1789, for the Court has said that "at the absolute minimum" the Clause protects the writ as it existed when the Constitution was drafted and ratified.

To support their arguments, the parties in these cases have examined historical sources to construct a view of the common-law writ as it existed in 1789—as have amici whose expertise in legal history the Court has relied upon in the past. Diligent search by all parties reveals no certain conclusions. In none of the cases cited do we find that a common-law court would or would not have granted, or refused to hear for lack of jurisdiction, a petition for a writ of habeas corpus brought by a prisoner deemed an enemy combatant, under a standard like the one the Department of Defense has used in these cases, and when held in a territory, like Guantanamo, over which the Government has total military and civil control.

Both arguments are premised, however, upon the assumption that the historical record is complete and that the common law, if properly understood, yields a definite answer to the questions before us. There are reasons to doubt both assumptions. Recent scholarship points to the inherent shortcomings in the historical record. And given the unique status of Guantanamo Bay and the particular dangers of terrorism in the modern age, the common-law courts simply may not have confronted cases with close parallels to this one. We decline, therefore, to infer too much, one way or the other, from the lack of historical evidence on point. Cf. Brown v. Board of Education (1954) (noting evidence concerning the circumstances surrounding the adoption of the Fourteenth Amendment, discussed in the parties' briefs and uncovered through the Court's own investigation, "convince us that, although these sources cast some light, it is not enough to resolve the problem with which we are faced. At best, they are inconclusive").

IV

Drawing from its position that at common law the writ ran only to territories over which the Crown was sovereign, the Government says the Suspension Clause affords petitioners no rights because the United States does not claim sovereignty over the place of detention.

Guantanamo Bay is not formally part of the United States. And under the terms of the lease between the United States and Cuba, Cuba retains "ultimate sovereignty" over the territory while the United States exercises "complete jurisdiction and control." Under the terms of the 1934 Treaty, however, Cuba effectively has no rights as a sovereign until the parties agree to modification of the 1903 Lease Agreement or the United States abandons the base.

The United States contends, nevertheless, that Guantanamo is not within its sovereign control. This was the Government's position well before the events of September 11, 2001. And in other contexts the Court has held that questions of sovereignty are for the political branches to decide. Even if this were a treaty interpretation case that did not involve a political question, the President's construction of the lease agreement would be entitled to great respect.

We therefore do not question the Government's position that Cuba, not the United States, maintains sovereignty, in the legal and technical sense of the term, over Guantanamo Bay. But this does not end the analysis. Our cases do not hold it is improper for us to inquire into the objective degree of control the Nation asserts over foreign territory. Accordingly, for purposes of our analysis, we accept the Government's position that Cuba, and not the United States, retains de jure sovereignty over Guantanamo Bay. As we did in Rasul, however, we take notice of the obvious and uncontested fact that the United States, by virtue of its complete jurisdiction and control over the base, maintains de facto sovereignty over this territory.

Were we to hold that the present cases turn on the political question doctrine, we would be required first to accept the Government's premise that de jure sovereignty is the touchstone of habeas corpus jurisdiction. This premise, however, is unfounded. For the reasons indicated above, the history of common-law habeas corpus provides scant support for this proposition; and, for the reasons indicated below, that position would be inconsistent with our precedents and contrary to fundamental separation-of-powers principles.

A

The Court has discussed the issue of the Constitution's extraterritorial application on many occasions. These decisions undermine the Government's argument that, at least as applied to noncitizens, the Constitution necessarily stops where de jure sovereignty ends.

Practical considerations weighed heavily as well in Johnson v. Eisentrager (1950), where the Court addressed whether habeas corpus jurisdiction extended to enemy aliens who had been convicted of violating the laws of war. The prisoners were detained at Landsberg Prison in Germany during the Allied Powers' postwar occupation. The Court stressed the difficulties of ordering the Government to produce the prisoners in a habeas corpus proceeding. It "would require allocation of shipping space, guarding personnel, billeting and rations" and would damage the prestige of military commanders at a sensitive time.

True, the Court in Eisentrager denied access to the writ, and it noted the prisoners "at no relevant time were within any territory over which the United States is sovereign, and [that] the scenes of their offense, their capture, their trial and their punishment were all beyond the territorial jurisdiction of any court of the United States." The Government seizes upon this language as proof positive that the Eisentrager Court adopted a formalistic, sovereignty-based test for determining the reach of the Suspension Clause. We reject this reading for three reasons.

First, we do not accept the idea that the above-quoted passage from Eisentrager is the only authoritative language in the opinion and that all the rest is dicta. The Court's further determinations, based on practical considerations, were integral to Part II of its opinion and came before the decision announced its holding.

Second, because the United States lacked both de jure sovereignty and plenary control over Landsberg Prison, it is far from clear that the Eisentrager Court used the term sovereignty only in the narrow technical sense and not to connote the degree of control the military asserted over the facility. The Justices who decided Eisentrager would have understood sovereignty as a multifaceted concept. That the Court devoted a significant portion of Part II to a discussion of practical barriers to the running of the writ suggests that the Court was not concerned exclusively with the formal legal status of Landsberg Prison but also with the objective degree of control the United States asserted over it. Even if we assume the Eisentrager Court considered the United States' lack of formal legal sovereignty over Landsberg Prison as the decisive factor in that case, its holding is not inconsistent with a functional approach to questions of extraterritoriality.

Habeas Corpus

The formal legal status of a given territory affects, at least to some extent, the political branches' control over that territory. De jure sovereignty is a factor that bears upon which constitutional guarantees apply there.

Third, if the Government's reading of Eisentrager were correct, the opinion would have marked not only a change in, but a complete repudiation of, the Insular Cases' functional approach to questions of extraterritoriality. We cannot accept the Government's view. Nothing in Eisentrager says that de jure sovereignty is or has ever been the only relevant consideration in determining the geographic reach of the Constitution or of habeas corpus.

B

The Government's formal sovereignty-based test raises troubling separation-of-powers concerns as well. The political history of Guantanamo illustrates the deficiencies of this approach. The United States has maintained complete and uninterrupted control of the bay for over 100 years. Yet the Government's view is that the Constitution had no effect there, at least as to noncitizens, because the United States disclaimed sovereignty in the formal sense of the term. The necessary implication of the argument is that by surrendering formal sovereignty over any unincorporated territory to a third party, while at the same time entering into a lease that grants total control over the territory back to the United States, it would be possible for the political branches to govern without legal constraint.

Our basic charter cannot be contracted away like this. Even when the United States acts outside its borders, its powers are not "absolute and unlimited" but are subject "to such restrictions as are expressed in the Constitution." Abstaining from questions involving formal sovereignty and territorial governance is one thing. To hold the political branches have the power to switch the Constitution on or off at will is quite another. The former position reflects this Court's recognition that certain matters requiring political judgments are best left to the political branches. The latter would permit a striking anomaly in our tripartite system of government, leading to a regime in which Congress and the President, not this Court, say "what the law is." Marbury v. Madison (1803).

These concerns have particular bearing upon the Suspension Clause question in the cases now before us, for the writ of habeas corpus is itself an indispensable mechanism for monitoring the separation of powers. The test for determining the scope of this provision must not be subject to manipulation by those whose power it is designed to restrain.

C

In addition to the practical concerns discussed above, the Eisentrager Court found relevant that each petitioner:

"(a) is an enemy alien; (b) has never been or resided in the United States; (c) was captured outside of our territory and there held in military custody as a prisoner of war; (d) was tried and convicted by a Military Commission sitting outside the United States; (e) for offenses against laws of war committed outside the United States; (f) and is at all times imprisoned outside the United States."

Based on this language from Eisentrager, and the reasoning in our other extraterritoriality opinions, we conclude that at least three factors are relevant in determining the reach of the Suspension Clause: (1) the citizenship and status of the detainee and the adequacy of the process through which that status determination was made; (2) the nature of the sites where apprehension and then detention took place; and (3) the practical obstacles inherent in resolving the prisoner's entitlement to the writ.

Applying this framework, we note at the onset that the status of these detainees is a matter of dispute. The petitioners, like those in Eisentrager, are not American citizens. But the petitioners in Eisentrager did not contest, it seems, the Court's assertion that they were "enemy alien[s]." In the instant cases, by contrast, the detainees deny they are enemy combatants. They have been afforded some process in CSRT proceedings to determine their status; but, unlike in Eisentrager, there has been no trial by military commission for violations of the laws of war. The difference is not trivial. The records from the Eisentrager trials suggest that, well before the petitioners brought their case to this Court, there had been a rigorous adversarial process to test the legality of their detention. The Eisentrager petitioners were charged by a bill of particulars that made detailed factual allegations against them. To rebut the accusations, they were entitled to representation by counsel, allowed to introduce evidence on their own behalf, and permitted to cross-examine the prosecution's witnesses.

In comparison the procedural protections afforded to the detainees in the CSRT hearings are far more limited, and, we conclude, fall well short of the procedures and adversarial mechanisms that would eliminate the need for habeas corpus review. Although the detainee is assigned a "Personal Representative" to assist him during CSRT proceedings, the Secretary of the Navy's memorandum makes clear that person is not the detainee's lawyer or even his "advocate." The Government's evidence is accorded a presumption of validity. The detainee is allowed to present "reasonably available" evidence, but his ability to rebut the Government's evidence against him is limited by the circumstances of his confinement and his lack of counsel at this stage. And although the detainee can seek review of his status determination in the Court of Appeals, that review process cannot cure all defects in the earlier proceedings.

As to the second factor relevant to this analysis, the detainees here are similarly situated to the Eisentrager petitioners in that the sites of their apprehension and detention are technically outside the sovereign territory of the United States. As noted earlier, this is a factor that weighs against finding they have rights under the Suspension Clause. But there are critical differences between Landsberg Prison, circa 1950, and the United States Naval Station at Guantanamo Bay in 2008. Unlike its present control over the naval station, the United States' control over the prison in Germany was neither absolute nor indefinite. Like all parts of occupied Germany, the prison was under the jurisdiction of the combined Allied

Forces. Guantanamo Bay, on the other hand, is no transient possession. In every practical sense Guantanamo is not abroad; it is within the constant jurisdiction of the United States.

As to the third factor, we recognize, as the Court did in Eisentrager, that there are costs to holding the Suspension Clause applicable in a case of military detention abroad. Habeas corpus proceedings may require expenditure of funds by the Government and may divert the attention of military personnel from other pressing tasks. While we are sensitive to these concerns, we do not find them dispositive. Compliance with any judicial process requires some incremental expenditure of resources. Yet civilian courts and the Armed Forces have functioned along side each other at various points in our history. The Government presents no credible arguments that the military mission at Guantanamo would be compromised if habeas corpus courts had jurisdiction to hear the detainees' claims. And in light of the plenary control the United States asserts over the base, none are apparent to us.

The situation in Eisentrager was far different, given the historical context and nature of the military's mission in post-War Germany. When hostilities in the European Theater came to an end, the United States became responsible for an occupation zone encompassing over 57,000 square miles with a population of 18 million. In addition to supervising massive reconstruction and aid efforts the American forces stationed in Germany faced potential security threats from a defeated enemy. In retrospect the post-War occupation may seem uneventful. But at the time Eisentrager was decided, the Court was right to be concerned about judicial interference with the military's efforts to contain "enemy elements, guerilla fighters, and 'were-wolves.'"

Similar threats are not apparent here; nor does the Government argue that they are. The United States Naval Station at Guantanamo Bay consists of 45 square miles of land and water. The base has been used, at various points, to house migrants and refugees temporarily. At present, however, other than the detainees themselves, the only long-term residents are American military personnel, their families, and a small number of workers. The detainees have been deemed enemies of the United States. At present, dangerous as they may be if released, they are contained in a secure prison facility located on an isolated and heavily fortified military base.

There is no indication, furthermore, that adjudicating a habeas corpus petition would cause friction with the host government. No Cuban court has jurisdiction over American military personnel at Guantanamo or the enemy combatants detained there. While obligated to abide by the terms of the lease, the United States is, for all practical purposes, answerable to no other sovereign for its acts on the base. Were that not the case, or if the detention facility were located in an active theater of war, arguments that issuing the writ would be "impracticable or anomalous" would have more weight. Under the facts presented here, however, there are few practical barriers to the running of the writ. To the extent barriers arise, habeas corpus procedures likely can be modified to address them.

We hold that Art. I, §9, cl. 2, of the Constitution has full effect at Guantanamo Bay. If the privilege of habeas corpus is to be denied to the detainees now before us, Congress must act in accordance with the requirements of the Suspension Clause.

V

In light of this holding the question becomes whether the statute stripping jurisdiction to issue the writ avoids the Suspension Clause mandate because Congress has provided adequate substitute procedures for habeas corpus.

The gravity of the separation-of-powers issues raised by these cases and the fact that these detainees have been denied meaningful access to a judicial forum for a period of years render these cases exceptional.

Our case law does not contain extensive discussion of standards defining suspension of the writ or of circumstances under which suspension has occurred. This simply confirms the care Congress has taken throughout our Nation's history to preserve the writ and its function. Indeed, most of the major legislative enactments pertaining to habeas corpus have acted not to contract the writ's protection but to expand it or to hasten resolution of prisoners' claims.

We do not endeavor to offer a comprehensive summary of the requisites for an adequate substitute for habeas corpus. We do consider it uncontroversial, however, that the privilege of habeas corpus entitles the prisoner to a meaningful opportunity to demonstrate that he is being held pursuant to "the erroneous application or interpretation" of relevant law. And the habeas court must have the power to order the conditional release of an individual unlawfully detained-though release need not be the exclusive remedy and is not the appropriate one in every case in which the writ is granted.

Where a person is detained by executive order, rather than, say, after being tried and convicted in a court, the need for collateral review is most pressing. A criminal conviction in the usual course occurs after a judicial hearing before a tribunal disinterested in the outcome and committed to procedures designed to ensure its own independence. These dynamics are not inherent in executive detention orders or executive review procedures. In this context the need for habeas corpus is more urgent. The intended duration of the detention and the reasons for it bear upon the precise scope of the inquiry. Habeas corpus proceedings need not resemble a criminal trial, even when the detention is by executive order. But the writ must be effective. The habeas court must have sufficient authority to conduct a meaningful review of both the cause for detention and the Executive's power to detain.

To determine the necessary scope of habeas corpus review, therefore, we must assess the CSRT process, the mechanism through which petitioners' designation as enemy combatants became final. Whether one characterizes the CSRT process as direct review of the Executive's battlefield determination that the detainee is an enemy combatant-as the parties have and as we do-or as the first step in the collateral review of a battlefield determination makes no difference in a proper analysis of whether the procedures Congress put in place are an adequate substitute for habeas corpus. What matters is the sum total of procedural protections afforded to the detainee at all stages, direct and collateral.

Petitioners identify what they see as myriad deficiencies in the CSRTs. The most relevant for our purposes are the constraints upon the detainee's ability to rebut the factual basis for the Government's assertion that he is an enemy combatant. As already noted, at the CSRT stage the detainee has limited means to find or present evidence to challenge the Government's case against him. He does not have the assistance of counsel and may not be aware of the most critical allegations that the Government relied upon to order his detention. The detainee can confront witnesses that testify during the CSRT proceedings. But given that there are in effect no limits on the admission of hearsay evidence-the only requirement is that the tribunal deem the evidence "relevant and helpful," the detainee's opportunity to question witnesses is likely to be more theoretical than real.

Even if we were to assume that the CSRTs satisfy due process standards, it would not end our inquiry. Habeas corpus is a collateral process that exists, in Justice Holmes' words, to "cu[t] through all forms and g[o] to the very tissue of the structure. It comes in from the outside, not in subordination to the proceedings, and although every form may have been preserved opens the inquiry whether they have been more than an empty shell." Even when the procedures authorizing detention are structurally sound, the Suspension Clause remains applicable and the writ relevant.

Although we make no judgment as to whether the CSRTs, as currently constituted, satisfy due process standards, we agree with petitioners that, even when all the parties involved in this process act with diligence and in good faith, there is considerable risk of error in the tribunal's findings of fact. And given that the consequence of error may be detention of persons for the duration of hostilities that may last a generation or more, this is a risk too significant to ignore.

For the writ of habeas corpus, or its substitute, to function as an effective and proper remedy in this context, the court that conducts the habeas proceeding must have the means to correct errors that occurred during the CSRT proceedings. This includes some authority to assess the sufficiency of the Government's evidence against the detainee. It also must have the authority to admit and consider relevant exculpatory evidence that was not introduced during the earlier proceeding. Federal habeas petitioners long have had the means to supplement the record on review, even in the postconviction habeas setting. Here that opportunity is constitutionally required.

The extent of the showing required of the Government in these cases is a matter to be determined. We need not explore it further at this stage. We do hold that when the judicial power to issue habeas corpus properly is invoked the judicial officer must have adequate authority to make a determination in light of the relevant law and facts and to formulate and issue appropriate orders for relief, including, if necessary, an order directing the prisoner's release.

C

We now consider whether the DTA allows the Court of Appeals to conduct a proceeding meeting these standards. The DTA does not explicitly empower the Court of Appeals to order the applicant in a DTA review proceeding released should the court find that the standards and procedures used at his CSRT hearing were insufficient to justify detention. This is troubling. Yet, for present purposes, we can assume congressional silence permits a constitutionally required remedy.

The absence of a release remedy and specific language allowing AUMF challenges are not the only constitutional infirmities from which the statute potentially suffers, however. The more difficult question is whether the DTA permits the Court of Appeals to make requisite findings of fact. Assuming the DTA can be construed to allow the Court of Appeals to review or correct the CSRT's factual determinations, as opposed to merely certifying that the tribunal applied the correct standard of proof, we see no way to construe the statute to allow what is also constitutionally required in this context: an opportunity for the detainee to present relevant exculpatory evidence that was not made part of the record in the earlier proceedings.

On its face the statute allows the Court of Appeals to consider no evidence outside the CSRT record. Under the DTA the Court of Appeals has the power to review CSRT determinations by assessing the legality of standards and procedures. This implies the power to inquire into what happened at the CSRT hearing and, perhaps, to remedy certain deficiencies in that proceeding. But should the Court of Appeals determine that the CSRT followed appropriate and lawful standards and procedures, it will have reached the limits of its jurisdiction. There is no language in the DTA that can be construed to allow the Court of Appeals to admit and consider newly discovered evidence that could not have been made part of the CSRT record because it was unavailable to either the Government or the detainee when the CSRT made its findings. This evidence, however, may be critical to the detainee's argument that he is not an enemy combatant and there is no cause to detain him.

By foreclosing consideration of evidence not presented or reasonably available to the detainee at the CSRT proceedings, the DTA disadvantages the detainee by limiting the scope of collateral review to a record that may not be accurate or complete.

Although we do not hold that an adequate substitute must duplicate §2241 in all respects, it suffices that the Government has not established that the detainees' access to the statutory review provisions at issue is an adequate substitute for the writ of habeas corpus. MCA §7 thus effects an unconstitutional suspension of the writ. In view of our holding we need not discuss the reach of the writ with respect to claims of unlawful conditions of treatment or confinement.

VI

The real risks, the real threats, of terrorist attacks are constant and not likely soon to abate. The ways to disrupt our life and laws are so many and unforeseen that the Court should not attempt even some general catalogue of crises that might occur. Certain principles are apparent, however. Practical considerations and exigent circumstances inform the definition and reach of the law's writs, including habeas corpus. The cases and our tradition reflect this precept.

In cases involving foreign citizens detained abroad by the Executive, it likely would be both an impractical and unprecedented extension of judicial power to assume that habeas corpus would be available at the moment the prisoner is taken into custody. If and when habeas corpus jurisdiction applies, as it does in these cases, then proper deference can be accorded to reasonable procedures for screening and initial detention under lawful and proper conditions of confinement and treatment for a reasonable period of time. Domestic exigencies, furthermore, might also impose such onerous burdens on the Government that here, too, the Judicial Branch would be required to devise sensible rules for staying habeas corpus proceedings until the Government can comply with its requirements in a responsible way. Here, as is true with detainees apprehended abroad, a relevant consideration in determining the courts' role is whether there are suitable alternative processes in place to protect against the arbitrary exercise of governmental power.

The cases before us, however, do not involve detainees who have been held for a short period of time while awaiting their CSRT determinations. Were that the case, or were it probable that the Court of Appeals could complete a prompt review of their applications, the case for requiring temporary abstention or exhaustion of alternative remedies would be much stronger. These qualifications no longer pertain here. In some of these cases six years have elapsed without the judicial oversight that habeas corpus or an adequate substitute demands. And there has been no showing that the Executive faces such onerous burdens that it cannot respond to habeas corpus actions. To require these detainees to complete DTA review before proceeding with their habeas corpus actions would be to require additional months, if not years, of delay. The detainees in these cases are entitled to a prompt habeas corpus hearing.

Our decision today holds only that the petitioners before us are entitled to seek the writ; that the DTA review procedures are an inadequate substitute for habeas corpus; and that the petitioners in these cases need not exhaust the review procedures in the Court of Appeals before proceeding with their habeas actions in the District Court. The only law we identify as unconstitutional is MCA §7. Accordingly, both the DTA and the CSRT process remain intact. Our holding with regard to exhaustion should not be read to imply that a habeas court should intervene the moment an enemy combatant steps foot in a territory where the writ runs. The Executive is entitled to a reasonable period of time to determine a detainee's status before a court entertains that detainee's habeas corpus petition.

In considering both the procedural and substantive standards used to impose detention to prevent acts of terrorism, proper deference must be accorded to the political branches. There are further considerations, however. Security subsists, too, in fidelity to freedom's first principles. Chief among these are freedom from arbitrary and unlawful restraint and the personal liberty that is secured by adherence to the separation of powers. It is from these principles that the judicial authority to consider petitions for habeas corpus relief derives.

Our opinion does not undermine the Executive's powers as Commander in Chief. On the contrary, the exercise of those powers is vindicated, not eroded, when confirmed by the Judicial Branch. Within the Constitution's separation-of-powers structure, few exercises of judicial power are as legitimate or as necessary as the responsibility to hear challenges to the authority of the Executive to imprison a person. Some of these petitioners have been in custody for six years with no definitive judicial determination as to the legality of their detention. Their access to the writ is a necessity to determine the lawfulness of their status, even if, in the end, they do not obtain the relief they seek.

Because our Nation's past military conflicts have been of limited duration, it has been possible to leave the outer boundaries of war powers undefined. If, as some fear, terrorism continues to pose dangerous threats to us for years to come, the Court might not have this luxury. This result is not inevitable, however. The political branches, consistent with their independent obligations to interpret and uphold the Constitution, can engage in a genuine debate about how best to preserve constitutional values while protecting the Nation from terrorism.

It bears repeating that our opinion does not address the content of the law that governs petitioners' detention. That is a matter yet to be determined. We hold that petitioners may invoke the fundamental procedural protections of habeas corpus. The laws and Constitution are designed to survive, and remain in force, in extraordinary times. Liberty and security can be reconciled; and in our system they are reconciled within the framework of the law. The Framers decided that habeas corpus, a right of first importance, must be a part of that framework, a part of that law.

Justice SOUTER, with whom Justice GINSBURG and Justice BREYER join, concurring.

I join the Court's opinion in its entirety and add this afterword only to emphasize two things one might overlook after reading the dissents.

Four years ago, this Court in Rasul v. Bush (2004) held that statutory habeas jurisdiction extended to claims of foreign nationals imprisoned by the United States at Guantanamo Bay, "to determine the legality of the Executive's potentially indefinite detention" of them. Subsequent legislation eliminated the statutory habeas jurisdiction over these claims, so that now there must be constitutionally based jurisdiction or none at all. But no one who reads the Court's opinion in Rasul could seriously doubt that the jurisdictional question must be answered the same way in purely constitutional cases, given the Court's reliance on the historical background of habeas generally in answering the statutory question.

A second fact insufficiently appreciated by the dissents is the length of the disputed imprisonments, some of the prisoners represented here today having been locked up for six years. Hence the hollow ring when the dissenters suggest that the Court is somehow precipitating the judiciary into reviewing claims that the military (subject to appeal to the Court of Appeals for the District of Columbia Circuit) could handle within some reasonable period of time. These suggestions of judicial haste are all the more out of place given the Court's realistic acknowledgment that in periods of exigency the tempo of any habeas review must reflect the immediate peril facing the country. After six years of sustained executive detentions in Guantanamo, subject to habeas jurisdiction but without any actual habeas scrutiny, today's decision is no judicial victory, but an act of perseverance in trying to make habeas review, and the obligation of the courts to provide it, mean something of value both to prisoners and to the Nation.

CHIEF JUSTICE ROBERTS, with whom Justice SCALIA, Justice THOMAS, and Justice ALITO join, dissenting.

Today the Court strikes down as inadequate the most generous set of procedural protections ever afforded aliens detained by this country as enemy combatants. The political branches crafted these procedures amidst an ongoing military conflict, after much careful investigation and thorough debate. The Court rejects them today out of hand, without bothering to say what due process rights the detainees possess, without explaining how the statute fails to vindicate those rights, and before a single petitioner has even attempted to avail himself of the law's operation. And to what effect? The majority merely replaces a review system designed by the people's representatives with a set of shapeless procedures to be defined by federal courts at some future date. One cannot help but think, after surveying the modest practical results of the majority's ambitious opinion, that this decision is not really about the detainees at all, but about control of federal policy regarding enemy combatants.

The majority is adamant that the Guantanamo detainees are entitled to the protections of habeas corpus-its opinion begins by deciding that question. I regard the issue as a difficult one, primarily because of the unique and unusual jurisdictional status of Guantanamo Bay. I nonetheless agree with Justice Scalia's analysis of our precedents and the pertinent history of the writ, and accordingly join his dissent. The important point for me, however, is that the Court should have resolved these cases on other grounds. Habeas is most fundamentally a procedural right, a mechanism for contesting the legality of executive detention. The critical threshold question in these cases, prior to any inquiry about the writ's scope, is whether the system the political branches designed protects whatever rights the detainees may possess. If so, there is no need for any additional process, whether called "habeas" or something else.

Congress entrusted that threshold question in the first instance to the Court of Appeals for the District of Columbia Circuit, as the Constitution surely allows Congress to do. But before the D.C. Circuit has addressed the issue, the Court cashiers the statute, and without answering this critical threshold question itself. The Court does eventually get around to asking whether review under the DTA is, as the Court frames it, an "adequate substitute" for habeas, but even then its opinion fails to determine what rights the detainees possess and whether the DTA system satisfies them. The majority instead compares the undefined DTA process to an equally undefined habeas right-one that is to be given shape only in the future by district courts on a case-by-case basis. This whole approach is misguided.

It is also fruitless. How the detainees' claims will be decided now that the DTA is gone is anybody's guess. But the habeas process the Court mandates will most likely end up looking a lot like the DTA system it replaces, as the district court judges shaping it will have to reconcile review of the prisoners' detention with the undoubted need to protect the American people from the terrorist threat-precisely the challenge Congress undertook in drafting the DTA. All that today's opinion has done is shift responsibility for those sensitive foreign policy and national security decisions from the elected branches to the Federal Judiciary.

I believe the system the political branches constructed adequately protects any constitutional rights aliens captured abroad and detained as enemy combatants may enjoy. I therefore would dismiss these cases on that ground. With all respect for the contrary views of the majority, I must dissent.

The majority's overreaching is particularly egregious given the weakness of its objections to the DTA. Simply put, the Court's opinion fails on its own terms. The majority strikes down the statute because it is not an "adequate substitute" for habeas review, but fails to show what rights the detainees have that cannot be vindicated by the DTA system.

Because the central purpose of habeas corpus is to test the legality of executive detention, the writ requires most fundamentally an Article III court able to hear the prisoner's claims and, when necessary, order release. Beyond that, the process a given prisoner is entitled to receive depends on the circumstances and the rights of the prisoner. After much hemming and hawing, the majority appears to concede that the DTA provides an Article III court competent to order release. The only issue in dispute is the process the Guantanamo prisoners are entitled to use to test the legality of their detention. Hamdi concluded that American citizens detained as enemy combatants are entitled to only limited process, and that much of that process could be supplied by a military tribunal, with review to follow in an Article III court. That is precisely the system we have here. It is adequate to vindicate whatever due process rights petitioners may have.

The Court reaches the opposite conclusion partly because it misreads the statute. The majority appears not to understand how the review system it invalidates actually works-specifically, how CSRT review and review by the D.C. Circuit fit together. After briefly acknowledging in its recitation of the facts that the Government designed the CSRTs "to comply with the due process requirements identified by the plurality in Hamdi," the Court proceeds to dismiss the tribunal proceedings as no more than a suspect method used by the Executive for determining the status of the detainees in the first instance.

The majority is equally wrong to characterize the CSRTs as part of that initial determination process. They are instead a means for detainees to challenge the Government's determination. The Executive designed the CSRTs to mirror Army

Habeas Corpus

Regulation 190-8, the very procedural model the plurality in Hamdi said provided the type of process an enemy combatant could expect from a habeas court. The CSRTs operate much as habeas courts would if hearing the detainee's collateral challenge for the first time: They gather evidence, call witnesses, take testimony, and render a decision on the legality of the Government's detention. If the CSRT finds a particular detainee has been improperly held, it can order release.

The majority insists that even if "the CSRTs satisf[ied] due process standards," full habeas review would still be necessary, because habeas is a collateral remedy available even to prisoners "detained pursuant to the most rigorous proceedings imaginable." This comment makes sense only if the CSRTs are incorrectly viewed as a method used by the Executive for determining the prisoners' status, and not as themselves part of the collateral review to test the validity of that determination. The majority can deprecate the importance of the CSRTs only by treating them as something they are not.

In short, the Hamdi plurality concluded that this type of review would be enough to satisfy due process, even for citizens. Congress followed the Court's lead, only to find itself the victim of a constitutional bait and switch.

Given the statutory scheme the political branches adopted, and given Hamdi, it simply will not do for the majority to dismiss the CSRT procedures as "far more limited" than those used in military trials, and therefore beneath the level of process "that would eliminate the need for habeas corpus review." The question is not how much process the CSRTs provide in comparison to other modes of adjudication. The question is whether the CSRT procedures-coupled with the judicial review specified by the DTA-provide the "basic process" Hamdi said the Constitution affords American citizens detained as enemy combatants.

To what basic process are these detainees due as habeas petitioners? We have said that "at the absolute minimum," the Suspension Clause protects the writ "'as it existed in 1789.'" The majority admits that a number of historical authorities suggest that at the time of the Constitution's ratification, "common-law courts abstained altogether from matters involving prisoners of war." If this is accurate, the process provided prisoners under the DTA is plainly more than sufficient-it allows alleged combatants to challenge both the factual and legal bases of their detentions.

Assuming the constitutional baseline is more robust, the DTA still provides adequate process, and by the majority's own standards. The DTA system-CSRT review of the Executive's determination followed by D.C. Circuit review for sufficiency of the evidence and the constitutionality of the CSRT process-meets these criteria.

All told, the DTA provides the prisoners held at Guantanamo Bay adequate opportunity to contest the bases of their detentions, which is all habeas corpus need allow. The DTA provides more opportunity and more process, in fact, than that afforded prisoners of war or any other alleged enemy combatants in history.

Despite these guarantees, the Court finds the DTA system an inadequate habeas substitute, for one central reason: Detainees are unable to introduce at the appeal stage exculpatory evidence discovered after the conclusion of their CSRT proceedings. The Court hints darkly that the DTA may suffer from other infirmities, but it does not bother to name them, making a response a bit difficult. As it stands, I can only assume the Court regards the supposed defect it did identify as the gravest of the lot.

If this is the most the Court can muster, the ice beneath its feet is thin indeed. As noted, the CSRT procedures provide ample opportunity for detainees to introduce exculpatory evidence-whether documentary in nature or from live witnesses-before the military tribunals. And if their ability to introduce such evidence is denied contrary to the Constitution or laws of the United States, the D.C. Circuit has the authority to say so on review.

For all its eloquence about the detainees' right to the writ, the Court makes no effort to elaborate how exactly the remedy it prescribes will differ from the procedural protections detainees enjoy under the DTA. The Court objects to the detainees' limited access to witnesses and classified material, but proposes no alternatives of its own. Indeed, it simply ignores the many difficult questions its holding presents. What, for example, will become of the CSRT process? The majority says federal courts should generally refrain from entertaining detainee challenges until after the petitioner's CSRT proceeding has finished. But to what deference, if any, is that CSRT determination entitled?

There are other problems. Take witness availability. What makes the majority think witnesses will become magically available when the review procedure is labeled "habeas"? Will the location of most of these witnesses change-will they suddenly become easily susceptible to service of process? Or will subpoenas issued by American habeas courts run to Basra? And if they did, how would they be enforced? Speaking of witnesses, will detainees be able to call active-duty military officers as witnesses? If not, why not?

The majority has no answers for these difficulties. What it does say leaves open the distinct possibility that its "habeas" remedy will, when all is said and done, end up looking a great deal like the DTA review it rejects.

The majority rests its decision on abstract and hypothetical concerns. Step back and consider what, in the real world, Congress and the Executive have actually granted aliens captured by our Armed Forces overseas and found to be enemy combatants:

- The right to hear the bases of the charges against them, including a summary of any classified evidence.
- The ability to challenge the bases of their detention before military tribunals modeled after Geneva Convention procedures. Some 38 detainees have been released as a result of this process.
- The right, before the CSRT, to testify, introduce evidence, call witnesses, question those the Government calls, and secure release, if and when appropriate.

- The right to the aid of a personal representative in arranging and presenting their cases before a CSRT.
- Before the D.C. Circuit, the right to employ counsel, challenge the factual record, contest the lower tribunal's legal determinations, ensure compliance with the Constitution and laws, and secure release, if any errors below establish their entitlement to such relief.

In sum, the DTA satisfies the majority's own criteria for assessing adequacy. This statutory scheme provides the combatants held at Guantanamo greater procedural protections than have ever been afforded alleged enemy detainees-whether citizens or aliens-in our national history.

So who has won? Not the detainees. The Court's analysis leaves them with only the prospect of further litigation to determine the content of their new habeas right, followed by further litigation to resolve their particular cases, followed by further litigation before the D.C. Circuit—where they could have started had they invoked the DTA procedure. Not Congress, whose attempt to "determine—through democratic means—how best" to balance the security of the American people with the detainees' liberty interests, has been unceremoniously brushed aside. Not the Great Writ, whose majesty is hardly enhanced by its extension to a jurisdictionally quirky outpost, with no tangible benefit to anyone. Not the rule of law, unless by that is meant the rule of lawyers, who will now arguably have a greater role than military and intelligence officials in shaping policy for alien enemy combatants. And certainly not the American people, who today lose a bit more control over the conduct of this Nation's foreign policy to unelected, politically unaccountable judges.

Justice SCALIA, with whom THE CHIEF JUSTICE, Justice THOMAS, and Justice ALITO join, dissenting.

Today, for the first time in our Nation's history, the Court confers a constitutional right to habeas corpus on alien enemies detained abroad by our military forces in the course of an ongoing war. The Chief Justice's dissent, which I join, shows that the procedures prescribed by Congress in the Detainee Treatment Act provide the essential protections that habeas corpus guarantees; there has thus been no suspension of the writ, and no basis exists for judicial intervention beyond what the Act allows. My problem with today's opinion is more fundamental still: The writ of habeas corpus does not, and never has, run in favor of aliens abroad; the Suspension Clause thus has no application, and the Court's intervention in this military matter is entirely ultra vires.

I shall devote most of what will be a lengthy opinion to the legal errors contained in the opinion of the Court. Contrary to my usual practice, however, I think it appropriate to begin with a description of the disastrous consequences of what the Court has done today.

America is at war with radical Islamists. The enemy began by killing Americans and American allies abroad: 241 at the Marine barracks in Lebanon,

19 at the Khobar Towers in Dhahran, 224 at our embassies in Dar es Salaam and Nairobi, and 17 on the USS Cole in Yemen. On September 11, 2001, the enemy brought the battle to American soil, killing 2,749 at the Twin Towers in New York City, 184 at the Pentagon in Washington, D. C., and 40 in Pennsylvania. It has threatened further attacks against our homeland; one need only walk about buttressed and barricaded Washington, or board a plane anywhere in the country, to know that the threat is a serious one. Our Armed Forces are now in the field against the enemy, in Afghanistan and Iraq. Last week, 13 of our countrymen in arms were killed.

The game of bait-and-switch that today's opinion plays upon the Nation's Commander in Chief will make the war harder on us. It will almost certainly cause more Americans to be killed. That consequence would be tolerable if necessary to preserve a time-honored legal principle vital to our constitutional Republic. But it is this Court's blatant abandonment of such a principle that produces the decision today. The President relied on our settled precedent in Johnson v. Eisentrager (1950), when he established the prison at Guantanamo Bay for enemy aliens. Citing that case, the President's Office of Legal Counsel advised him "that the great weight of legal authority indicates that a federal district court could not properly exercise habeas jurisdiction over an alien detained at [Guantanamo Bay]." Memorandum from Patrick F. Philbin and John C. Yoo, Deputy Assistant Attorneys General, Office of Legal Counsel, to William J. Haynes II, General Counsel, Dept. of Defense (Dec. 28, 2001). Had the law been otherwise, the military surely would not have transported prisoners there, but would have kept them in Afghanistan, transferred them to another of our foreign military bases, or turned them over to allies for detention. Those other facilities might well have been worse for the detainees themselves.

In the long term, then, the Court's decision today accomplishes little, except perhaps to reduce the well-being of enemy combatants that the Court ostensibly seeks to protect. In the short term, however, the decision is devastating. At least 30 of those prisoners hitherto released from Guantanamo Bay have returned to the battlefield. See S.Rep. No. 110-90, pt. 7, p. 13 (2007) (Minority Views of Sens. Kyl, Sessions, Graham, Cornyn, and Coburn) (hereinafter Minority Report). Some have been captured or killed. See also Mintz, Released Detainees Rejoining the Fight, Washington Post, Oct. 22, 2004, pp. A1, A12. But others have succeeded in carrying on their atrocities against innocent civilians. In one case, a detainee released from Guantanamo Bay masterminded the kidnapping of two Chinese dam workers, one of whom was later shot to death when used as a human shield against Pakistani commandoes. Another former detainee promptly resumed his post as a senior Taliban commander and murdered a United Nations engineer and three Afghan soldiers. Mintz, supra. Still another murdered an Afghan judge. It was reported only last month that a released detainee carried out a suicide bombing against Iraqi soldiers in Mosul, Iraq. See White, Ex-Guantanamo Detainee Joined Iraq Suicide Attack, Washington Post, May 8, 2008, p. A18.

These, mind you, were detainees whom the military had concluded were not enemy combatants. Their return to the kill illustrates the incredible difficulty of assessing who is and who is not an enemy combatant in a foreign theater of operations where the environment does not lend itself to rigorous evidence collection. Astoundingly, the Court today raises the bar, requiring military officials to appear before civilian courts and defend their decisions under procedural and evidentiary rules that go beyond what Congress has specified. As The Chief Justice's dissent makes clear, we have no idea what those procedural and evidentiary rules are, but they will be determined by civil courts and (in the Court's contemplation at least) will be more detainee-friendly than those now applied, since otherwise there would no reason to hold the congressionally prescribed procedures unconstitutional. If they impose a higher standard of proof (from foreign battlefields) than the current procedures require, the number of the enemy returned to combat will obviously increase.

But even when the military has evidence that it can bring forward, it is often foolhardy to release that evidence to the attorneys representing our enemies. And one escalation of procedures that the Court is clear about is affording the detainees increased access to witnesses (perhaps troops serving in Afghanistan?) and to classified information. During the 1995 prosecution of Omar Abdel Rahman, federal prosecutors gave the names of 200 unindicted co-conspirators to the "Blind Sheik's" defense lawyers; that information was in the hands of Osama Bin Laden within two weeks. In another case, trial testimony revealed to the enemy that the United States had been monitoring their cellular network, whereupon they promptly stopped using it, enabling more of them to evade capture and continue their atrocities.

And today it is not just the military that the Court elbows aside. A mere two Terms ago in Hamdan v. Rumsfeld (2006), when the Court held (quite amazingly) that the Detainee Treatment Act of 2005 had not stripped habeas jurisdiction over Guantanamo petitioners' claims, four Members of today's five-Justice majority joined an opinion saying the following: "Nothing prevents the President from returning to Congress to seek the authority [for trial by military commission] he believes necessary."

Turns out they were just kidding. For in response, Congress, at the President's request, quickly enacted the Military Commissions Act, emphatically reasserting that it did not want these prisoners filing habeas petitions. It is therefore clear that Congress and the Executive—both political branches—have determined that limiting the role of civilian courts in adjudicating whether prisoners captured abroad are properly detained is important to success in the war that some 190,000 of our men and women are now fighting. As the Solicitor General argued, "the Military Commissions Act and the Detainee Treatment Act . . . represent an effort by the political branches to strike an appropriate balance between the need to preserve liberty and the need to accommodate the weighty and sensitive governmental interests in ensuring that those who have in fact fought with the enemy during a war do not return to battle against the United States."

But it does not matter. The Court today decrees that no good reason to accept the judgment of the other two branches is "apparent." "The Government," it declares, "presents no credible arguments that the military mission at Guantanamo would be compromised if habeas corpus courts had jurisdiction to hear the detainees' claims." What competence does the Court have to second-guess the judgment of Congress and the President on such a point? None whatever. But the Court blunders in nonetheless. Henceforth, as today's opinion makes unnervingly clear, how to handle enemy prisoners in this war will ultimately lie with the branch that knows least about the national security concerns that the subject entails.

Today the Court warps our Constitution in a way that goes beyond the narrow issue of the reach of the Suspension Clause, invoking judicially brainstormed separation-of-powers principles to establish a manipulable "functional" test for the extraterritorial reach of habeas corpus (and, no doubt, for the extraterritorial reach of other constitutional protections as well). It blatantly misdescribes important precedents, most conspicuously Justice Jackson's opinion for the Court in Johnson v. Eisentrager. It breaks a chain of precedent as old as the common law that prohibits judicial inquiry into detentions of aliens abroad absent statutory authorization. And, most tragically, it sets our military commanders the impossible task of proving to a civilian court, under whatever standards this Court devises in the future, that evidence supports the confinement of each and every enemy prisoner.

The Nation will live to regret what the Court has done today. I dissent.

FEDERAL RULES OF CRIMINAL PROCEDURE

Rule 5. Initial Appearance

(a) *In General.*

(1) Appearance Upon an Arrest.

(A) A person making an arrest within the United States must take the defendant without unnecessary delay before a magistrate judge, or before a state or local judicial officer as Rule 5(c) provides, unless a statute provides otherwise.

(B) A person making an arrest outside the United States must take the defendant without unnecessary delay before a magistrate judge, unless a statute provides otherwise.

(2) Exceptions.

(A) An officer making an arrest under a warrant issued upon a complaint charging solely a violation of 18 U.S.C. §1073 need not comply with this rule if:

(i) the person arrested is transferred without unnecessary delay to the custody of appropriate state or local authorities in the district of arrest; and

(ii) an attorney for the government moves promptly, in the district where the warrant was issued, to dismiss the complaint.

(B) If a defendant is arrested for violating probation or supervised release, Rule 32.1 applies.

(C) If a defendant is arrested for failing to appear in another district, Rule 40 applies.

(3) Appearance Upon a Summons.

When a defendant appears in response to a summons under Rule 4, a magistrate judge must proceed under Rule 5(d) or (e), as applicable.

(b)   Arrest Without a Warrant.

If a defendant is arrested without a warrant, a complaint meeting Rule 4(a)'s requirement of probable cause must be promptly filed in the district where the offense was allegedly committed.

(c)   Place of Initial Appearance; Transfer to Another District.

> (1)   Arrest in the District Where the Offense Was Allegedly Committed.

If the defendant is arrested in the district where the offense was allegedly committed:

(A) the initial appearance must be in that district; and

(B) if a magistrate judge is not reasonably available, the initial appearance may be before a state or local judicial officer.

> (2)   Arrest in a District Other Than Where the Offense Was Allegedly Committed.

If the defendant was arrested in a district other than where the offense was allegedly committed, the initial appearance must be:

(A) in the district of arrest; or

(B) in an adjacent district if:

(**i**) the appearance can occur more promptly there; or

(**ii**) the offense was allegedly committed there and the initial appearance will occur on the day of arrest.

> (3)   Procedures in a District Other Than Where the Offense Was Allegedly Committed.

(d)   Procedure in a Felony Case.

(1)   Advice.

If the defendant is charged with a felony, the judge must inform the defendant of the following:

(A) the complaint against the defendant, and any affidavit filed with it;

(B) the defendant's right to retain counsel or to request that counsel be appointed if the defendant cannot obtain counsel;

(C) the circumstances, if any, under which the defendant may secure pretrial release;

(D) any right to a preliminary hearing; and

(E) the defendant's right not to make a statement, and that any statement made may be used against the defendant.

(2)   Consulting with Counsel.

The judge must allow the defendant reasonable opportunity to consult with counsel.

(3)   Detention or Release.

The judge must detain or release the defendant as provided by statute or these rules.

(4)   Plea.

A defendant may be asked to plead only under Rule 10.

(e)   Procedure in a Misdemeanor Case.

If the defendant is charged with a misdemeanor only, the judge must inform the defendant in accordance with Rule 58(b)(2).

(f)   Video Teleconferencing.

Video teleconferencing may be used to conduct an appearance under this rule if the defendant consents.

Rule 5.1.   Preliminary Hearing

(a)   In General.

If a defendant is charged with an offense other than a petty offense, a magistrate judge must conduct a preliminary hearing unless:

(1) the defendant waives the hearing;

(2) the defendant is indicted;

(3) the government files an information under Rule 7(b) charging the defendant with a felony;

(4) the government files an information charging the defendant with a misdemeanor; or

(5) the defendant is charged with a misdemeanor and consents to trial before a magistrate judge.

(b)   Selecting a District.

A defendant arrested in a district other than where the offense was allegedly committed may elect to have the preliminary hearing conducted in the district where the prosecution is pending.

(c)   Scheduling.

The magistrate judge must hold the preliminary hearing within a reasonable time, but no later than 14 days after the initial appearance if the defendant is in custody and no later than 21 days if not in custody.

(d)   Extending the Time.

With the defendant's consent and upon a showing of good cause—taking into account the public interest in the prompt disposition of criminal cases—a magistrate judge may extend the time limits in Rule 5.1(c) one or more times. If the defendant does not consent, the magistrate judge may extend the time limits only on a showing that extraordinary circumstances exist and justice requires the delay.

(e) Hearing and Finding.

At the preliminary hearing, the defendant may cross-examine adverse witnesses and may introduce evidence but may not object to evidence on the ground that it was unlawfully acquired. If the magistrate judge finds probable cause to believe an offense has been committed and the defendant committed it, the magistrate judge must promptly require the defendant to appear for further proceedings.

(f) Discharging the Defendant.

If the magistrate judge finds no probable cause to believe an offense has been committed or the defendant committed it, the magistrate judge must dismiss the complaint and discharge the defendant. A discharge does not preclude the government from later prosecuting the defendant for the same offense.

(g) Recording the Proceedings.

The preliminary hearing must be recorded by a court reporter or by a suitable recording device. A recording of the proceeding may be made available to any party upon request. A copy of the recording and a transcript may be provided to any party upon request and upon any payment required by applicable Judicial Conference regulations.

(h) Producing a Statement.

(1) In General.

Rule 26.2(a)-(d) and (f) applies at any hearing under this rule, unless the magistrate judge for good cause rules otherwise in a particular case.

(2) Sanctions for Not Producing a Statement.

If a party disobeys a Rule 26.2 order to deliver a statement to the moving party, the magistrate judge must not consider the testimony of a witness whose statement is withheld.

Rule 6. The Grand Jury

(a) *Summoning a Grand Jury.*

(1) In General.

When the public interest so requires, the court must order that one or more grand juries be summoned. A grand jury must have 16 to 23 members, and the court must order that enough legally qualified persons be summoned to meet this requirement.

(2) Alternate Jurors.

When a grand jury is selected, the court may also select alternate jurors. Alternate jurors must have the same qualifications and be selected in the same manner as any other juror. Alternate jurors replace jurors in the same sequence in which the alternates were selected. An alternate juror who replaces a juror is subject to the same challenges, takes the same oath, and has the same authority as the other jurors.

(b) *Objection to the Grand Jury or to a Grand Juror.*

(1) Challenges.

Either the government or a defendant may challenge the grand jury on the ground that it was not lawfully drawn, summoned, or selected, and may challenge an individual juror on the ground that the juror is not legally qualified.

(2) Motion to Dismiss an Indictment.

A party may move to dismiss the indictment based on an objection to the grand jury or on an individual juror's lack of legal qualification, unless the court has previously ruled on the same objection under Rule 6(b)(1). The motion to dismiss is governed by 28 U.S.C. §1867(e). The court must not dismiss the indictment on the ground that a grand juror was not legally qualified if the record shows that at least 12 qualified jurors concurred in the indictment.

(c) *Foreperson and Deputy Foreperson.*

The court will appoint one juror as the foreperson and another as the deputy foreperson. In the foreperson's absence, the deputy foreperson will act as the foreperson. The foreperson may administer oaths and affirmations and will sign all indictments. The foreperson—or another juror designated by the foreperson—will record the number of jurors concurring in every indictment and will file the record with the clerk, but the record may not be made public unless the court so orders.

(d) Who May Be Present.

(1) While the Grand Jury Is in Session.

The following persons may be present while the grand jury is in session: attorneys for the government, the witness being questioned, interpreters when needed, and a court reporter or an operator of a recording device.

(2) During Deliberations and Voting.

No person other than the jurors, and any interpreter needed to assist a hearing-impaired or speech-impaired juror, may be present while the grand jury is deliberating or voting.

(e) Recording and Disclosing the Proceedings.

(1) Recording the Proceedings.

Except while the grand jury is deliberating or voting, all proceedings must be recorded by a court reporter or by a suitable recording device. But the validity of a prosecution is not affected by the unintentional failure to make a recording. Unless the court orders otherwise, an attorney for the government will retain control of the recording, the reporter's notes, and any transcript prepared from those notes.

(2) Secrecy.

(A) No obligation of secrecy may be imposed on any person except in accordance with Rule 6(e)(2)(B).

(B) Unless these rules provide otherwise, the following persons must not disclose a matter occurring before the grand jury:

(i) a grand juror;

(ii) an interpreter;

(iii) a court reporter;

(iv) an operator of a recording device;

(v) a person who transcribes recorded testimony;

(vi) an attorney for the government; or

(vii) a person to whom disclosure is made under Rule 6(e)(3)(A)(ii) or (iii).

(3)   Exceptions.

(A) Disclosure of a grand-jury matter—other than the grand jury's deliberations or any grand juror's vote—may be made to:

(i) an attorney for the government for use in performing that attorney's duty;

(ii) any government personnel—including those of a state, state subdivision, Indian tribe, or foreign government—that an attorney for the government considers necessary to assist in performing that attorney's duty to enforce federal criminal law; or

(iii) a person authorized by 18 U.S.C. §3322.

(B) A person to whom information is disclosed under Rule 6(e)(3)(A)(ii) may use that information only to assist an attorney for the government in performing that attorney's duty to enforce federal criminal law. An attorney for the government must promptly provide the court that impaneled the grand jury with the names of all persons to whom a disclosure has been made, and must certify that the attorney has advised those persons of their obligation of secrecy under this rule.

(C) An attorney for the government may disclose any grand-jury matter to another federal grand jury.

(D) An attorney for the government may disclose any grand-jury matter involving foreign intelligence, counterintelligence (as defined in 50 U.S.C. §401a), or foreign intelligence information (as defined in Rule 6(e)(3)(D)(iii)) to any federal law enforcement, intelligence, protective, immigration, national defense, or national security official to assist the official receiving the information in the performance of that official's duties. An attorney for the government may also disclose any grand-jury matter involving, within the United States or elsewhere, a threat of attack or other grave hostile acts of a foreign power or its agent, a threat of domestic or international sabotage or terrorism, or clandestine intelligence gathering activities by an intelligence service or network of a foreign power or by its agent, to any appropriate federal, state, state subdivision, Indian tribal, or foreign government official, for the purpose of preventing or responding to such threat or activities.

(i) Any official who receives information under Rule 6(e)(3)(D) may use the information only as necessary in the conduct of that person's official duties subject to any limitations on the unauthorized disclosure of such information. Any state, state subdivision, Indian tribal, or foreign government official who receives information under Rule 6(e)(3)(D) may use the information only in a manner consistent with any guidelines issued by the Attorney General and the Director of National Intelligence.

(ii) Within a reasonable time after disclosure is made under Rule 6(e)(3)(D), an attorney for the government must file, under seal, a notice with the court in the district where the grand jury convened stating that such information was disclosed and the departments, agencies, or entities to which the disclosure was made.

(iii) As used in Rule 6(e)(3)(D), the term "foreign intelligence information" means:

(a) information, whether or not it concerns a United States person, that relates to the ability of the United States to protect against—

- actual or potential attack or other grave hostile acts of a foreign power or its agent;
- sabotage or international terrorism by a foreign power or its agent; or
- clandestine intelligence activities by an intelligence service or network of a foreign power or by its agent; or

(b) information, whether or not it concerns a United States person, with respect to a foreign power or foreign territory that relates to—

- the national defense or the security of the United States; or
- the conduct of the foreign affairs of the United States.

(E) The court may authorize disclosure—at a time, in a manner, and subject to any other conditions that it directs—of a grand-jury matter:

(i) preliminarily to or in connection with a judicial proceeding;

(ii) at the request of a defendant who shows that a ground may exist to dismiss the indictment because of a matter that occurred before the grand jury;

(iii) at the request of the government, when sought by a foreign court or prosecutor for use in an official criminal investigation;

(iv) at the request of the government if it shows that the matter may disclose a violation of State, Indian tribal, or foreign criminal law, as long as the disclosure is to an appropriate state, state-subdivision, Indian tribal, or foreign government official for the purpose of enforcing that law; or

(v) at the request of the government if it shows that the matter may disclose a violation of military criminal law under the Uniform Code of Military Justice, as long as the disclosure is to an appropriate military official for the purpose of enforcing that law.

(F) A petition to disclose a grand-jury matter under Rule 6(e)(3)(E)(i) must be filed in the district where the grand jury convened. Unless the hearing is ex parte—as it may be when the government is the petitioner—the petitioner must serve the petition on, and the court must afford a reasonable opportunity to appear and be heard to:

(i) an attorney for the government;

(ii) the parties to the judicial proceeding; and

(iii) any other person whom the court may designate.

(G) If the petition to disclose arises out of a judicial proceeding in another district, the petitioned court must transfer the petition to the other court unless the petitioned court can reasonably determine whether disclosure is proper. If the petitioned court decides to transfer, it must send to the transferee court the material sought to be disclosed, if feasible, and a written evaluation of the need for continued grand-jury secrecy. The transferee court must afford those persons identified in Rule 6(e)(3)(F) a reasonable opportunity to appear and be heard.

(4)   Sealed Indictment.

The magistrate judge to whom an indictment is returned may direct that the indictment be kept secret until the defendant is in custody or has been released pending trial. The clerk must then seal the indictment, and no person may disclose the indictment's existence except as necessary to issue or execute a warrant or summons.

(5)   Closed Hearing.

Subject to any right to an open hearing in a contempt proceeding, the court must close any hearing to the extent necessary to prevent disclosure of a matter occurring before a grand jury.

(6)   Sealed Records.

Records, orders, and subpoenas relating to grand-jury proceedings must be kept under seal to the extent and as long as necessary to prevent the unauthorized disclosure of a matter occurring before a grand jury.

(7)   Contempt.

A knowing violation of Rule 6, or of any guidelines jointly issued by the Attorney General and the Director of National Intelligence under Rule 6, may be punished as a contempt of court.

(f)   Indictment and Return.

A grand jury may indict only if at least 12 jurors concur. The grand jury—or its foreperson or deputy foreperson—must return the indictment to a magistrate judge in open court. If a complaint or information is pending against the defendant and 12 jurors do not concur in the indictment, the foreperson must promptly and in writing report the lack of concurrence to the magistrate judge.

(g)   Discharging the Grand Jury.

A grand jury must serve until the court discharges it, but it may serve more than 18 months only if the court, having determined that an extension is in the public interest, extends the grand jury's service. An extension may be granted for no more than 6 months, except as otherwise provided by statute.

(h)   Excusing a Juror.

At any time, for good cause, the court may excuse a juror either temporarily or permanently, and if permanently, the court may impanel an alternate juror in place of the excused juror.

(i)   "Indian Tribe" Defined.

"Indian tribe" means an Indian tribe recognized by the Secretary of the Interior on a list published in the Federal Register under 25 U.S.C. §479a-1.

Rule 7.   The Indictment and the Information

(a)   When Used.

(1)   Felony.

An offense (other than criminal contempt) must be prosecuted by an indictment if it is punishable:

(A) by death; or

(B) by imprisonment for more than one year.

(2)   Misdemeanor.

An offense punishable by imprisonment for one year or less may be prosecuted in accordance with Rule 58(b)(1).

(b)   Waiving Indictment.

An offense punishable by imprisonment for more than one year may be prosecuted by information if the defendant—in open court and after being advised of the nature of the charge and of the defendant's rights—waives prosecution by indictment.

(c)   Nature and Contents.

(1)   In General.

The indictment or information must be a plain, concise, and definite written statement of the essential facts constituting the offense charged and must be signed by an attorney for the government. It need not contain a formal introduction or conclusion. A count may incorporate by reference an allegation made in another count. A count may allege that the means by which the defendant committed the offense are unknown or that the defendant committed it by one or more specified means. For each count, the indictment or information must give the official or customary citation of the statute, rule, regulation, or other provision of law that the defendant is alleged to have violated. For purposes of an indictment referred to in section 3282 of title 18, United States Code, for which the identity of the defendant is unknown, it shall be sufficient for the indictment to describe the defendant as an individual whose name is unknown, but who has a particular DNA profile, as that term is defined in that section 3282.

(2) Citation Error.

Unless the defendant was misled and thereby prejudiced, neither an error in a citation nor a citation's omission is a ground to dismiss the indictment or information or to reverse a conviction.

(d) Surplusage.

Upon the defendant's motion, the court may strike surplusage from the indictment or information.

(e) Amending an Information.

Unless an additional or different offense is charged or a substantial right of the defendant is prejudiced, the court may permit an information to be amended at any time before the verdict or finding.

(f) Bill of Particulars.

The court may direct the government to file a bill of particulars. The defendant may move for a bill of particulars before or within 14 days after arraignment or at a later time if the court permits. The government may amend a bill of particulars subject to such conditions as justice requires.

Rule 8. Joinder of Offenses or Defendants

(a) Joinder of Offenses.

The indictment or information may charge a defendant in separate counts with 2 or more offenses if the offenses charged—whether felonies or misdemeanors or both—are of the same or similar character, or are based on the same act or transaction, or are connected with or constitute parts of a common scheme or plan.

(b) Joinder of Defendants.

The indictment or information may charge 2 or more defendants if they are alleged to have participated in the same act or transaction, or in the same series of acts or transactions, constituting an offense or offenses. The defendants may be charged in one or more counts together or separately. All defendants need not be charged in each count.

Rule 11. Pleas

(a) Entering a Plea.

(1) In General.

A defendant may plead not guilty, guilty, or (with the court's consent) nolo contendere.

(2) Conditional Plea.

With the consent of the court and the government, a defendant may enter a conditional plea of guilty or nolo contendere, reserving in writing the right to have an appellate court review an adverse determination of a specified pretrial motion. A defendant who prevails on appeal may then withdraw the plea.

(3) Nolo Contendere Plea.

Before accepting a plea of nolo contendere, the court must consider the parties' views and the public interest in the effective administration of justice.

(4) Failure to Enter a Plea.

If a defendant refuses to enter a plea or if a defendant organization fails to appear, the court must enter a plea of not guilty.

(b) Considering and Accepting a Guilty or Nolo Contendere Plea.

(1) Advising and Questioning the Defendant.

Before the court accepts a plea of guilty or nolo contendere, the defendant may be placed under oath, and the court must address the defendant personally in open court. During this address, the court must inform the defendant of, and determine that the defendant understands, the following:

(A) the government's right, in a prosecution for perjury or false statement, to use against the defendant any statement that the defendant gives under oath;

(B) the right to plead not guilty, or having already so pleaded, to persist in that plea;

(C) the right to a jury trial;

(D) the right to be represented by counsel—and if necessary have the court appoint counsel—at trial and at every other stage of the proceeding;

(E) the right at trial to confront and cross-examine adverse witnesses, to be protected from compelled self-incrimination, to testify and present evidence, and to compel the attendance of witnesses;

(F) the defendant's waiver of these trial rights if the court accepts a plea of guilty or nolo contendere;

(G) the nature of each charge to which the defendant is pleading;

(H) any maximum possible penalty, including imprisonment, fine, and term of supervised release;

(I) any mandatory minimum penalty;

(J) any applicable forfeiture;

(K) the court's authority to order restitution;

(L) the court's obligation to impose a special assessment;

(M) in determining a sentence, the court's obligation to calculate the applicable sentencing-guideline range and to consider that range, possible departures under the Sentencing Guidelines, and other sentencing factors under 18 U.S.C. §3553(a); and

(N) the terms of any plea-agreement provision waiving the right to appeal or to collaterally attack the sentence.

(2)   Ensuring That a Plea Is Voluntary.

Before accepting a plea of guilty or nolo contendere, the court must address the defendant personally in open court and determine that the plea is voluntary and did not result from force, threats, or promises (other than promises in a plea agreement).

(3)   Determining the Factual Basis for a Plea.

Before entering judgment on a guilty plea, the court must determine that there is a factual basis for the plea.

(c)   *Plea Agreement Procedure.*

(1)   In General.

An attorney for the government and the defendant's attorney, or the defendant when proceeding pro se, may discuss and reach a plea agreement. The court must not participate in these discussions. If the defendant pleads guilty or nolo contendere to either a charged offense or a lesser or related offense, the plea agreement may specify that an attorney for the government will:

(A) not bring, or will move to dismiss, other charges;

(B) recommend, or agree not to oppose the defendant's request, that a particular sentence or sentencing range is appropriate or that a particular provision of the Sentencing Guidelines, or policy statement, or sentencing factor does or does not apply (such a recommendation or request does not bind the court); or

(C) agree that a specific sentence or sentencing range is the appropriate disposition of the case, or that a particular provision of the Sentencing Guidelines, or policy statement, or sentencing factor does or does not apply (such a recommendation or request binds the court once the court accepts the plea agreement).

(2)   Disclosing a Plea Agreement.

The parties must disclose the plea agreement in open court when the plea is offered, unless the court for good cause allows the parties to disclose the plea agreement in camera.

(3) Judicial Consideration of a Plea Agreement.

(A) To the extent the plea agreement is of the type specified in Rule 11(c)(1)(A) or (C), the court may accept the agreement, reject it, or defer a decision until the court has reviewed the presentence report.

(B) To the extent the plea agreement is of the type specified in Rule 11(c)(1)(B), the court must advise the defendant that the defendant has no right to withdraw the plea if the court does not follow the recommendation or request.

(4) Accepting a Plea Agreement.

If the court accepts the plea agreement, it must inform the defendant that to the extent the plea agreement is of the type specified in Rule 11(c)(1)(A) or (C), the agreed disposition will be included in the judgment.

(5) Rejecting a Plea Agreement.

If the court rejects a plea agreement containing provisions of the type specified in Rule 11(c)(1)(A) or (C), the court must do the following on the record and in open court (or, for good cause, in camera):

(A) inform the parties that the court rejects the plea agreement;

(B) advise the defendant personally that the court is not required to follow the plea agreement and give the defendant an opportunity to withdraw the plea; and

(C) advise the defendant personally that if the plea is not withdrawn, the court may dispose of the case less favorably toward the defendant than the plea agreement contemplated.

(d) *Withdrawing a Guilty or Nolo Contendere Plea.*

A defendant may withdraw a plea of guilty or nolo contendere:

(1) before the court accepts the plea, for any reason or no reason; or

(2) after the court accepts the plea, but before it imposes sentence if:

(A) the court rejects a plea agreement under Rule 11(c)(5); or

(B) the defendant can show a fair and just reason for requesting the withdrawal.

(e)   Finality of a Guilty or Nolo Contendere Plea.

After the court imposes sentence, the defendant may not withdraw a plea of guilty or nolo contendere, and the plea may be set aside only on direct appeal or collateral attack.

(f)   Admissibility or Inadmissibility of a Plea, Plea Discussions, and Related Statements.

The admissibility or inadmissibility of a plea, a plea discussion, and any related statement is governed by Federal Rule of Evidence 410.

(g)   Recording the Proceedings.

The proceedings during which the defendant enters a plea must be recorded by a court reporter or by a suitable recording device. If there is a guilty plea or a nolo contendere plea, the record must include the inquiries and advice to the defendant required under Rule 11(b) and (c).

(h)   Harmless Error.

A variance from the requirements of this rule is harmless error if it does not affect substantial rights.

Rule 14.   Relief from Prejudicial Joinder

(a)   Relief.

If the joinder of offenses or defendants in an indictment, an information, or a consolidation for trial appears to prejudice a defendant or the government, the court may order separate trials of counts, sever the defendants' trials, or provide any other relief that justice requires.

(b)   Defendant's Statements.

Before ruling on a defendant's motion to sever, the court may order an attorney for the government to deliver to the court for in camera inspection any defendant's statement that the government intends to use as evidence.

Rule 16.   Discovery and Inspection

(a)   *Government's Disclosure.*

(1)   Information Subject to Disclosure.

(A) Defendant's Oral Statement. Upon a defendant's request, the government must disclose to the defendant the substance of any relevant oral statement made by the defendant, before or after arrest, in response to interrogation by a person the defendant knew was a government agent if the government intends to use the statement at trial.

(B) Defendant's Written or Recorded Statement. Upon a defendant's request, the government must disclose to the defendant, and make available for inspection, copying, or photographing, all of the following:

(i) any relevant written or recorded statement by the defendant if:

- the statement is within the government's possession, custody, or control; and
- the attorney for the government knows—or through due diligence could know—that the statement exists;

(ii) the portion of any written record containing the substance of any relevant oral statement made before or after arrest if the defendant made the statement in response to interrogation by a person the defendant knew was a government agent; and

(iii) the defendant's recorded testimony before a grand jury relating to the charged offense.

(C) Organizational Defendant. Upon a defendant's request, if the defendant is an organization, the government must disclose to the defendant any statement described in Rule 16(a)(1)(A) and (B) if the government contends that the person making the statement:

(i) was legally able to bind the defendant regarding the subject of the statement because of that person's position as the defendant's director, officer, employee, or agent; or

(ii) was personally involved in the alleged conduct constituting the offense and was legally able to bind the defendant regarding that conduct because of that person's position as the defendant's director, officer, employee, or agent.

(D) Defendant's Prior Record. Upon a defendant's request, the government must furnish the defendant with a copy of the defendant's prior criminal record that is within the government's possession, custody, or control if the attorney for the government knows—or through due diligence could know—that the record exists.

(E) Documents and Objects. Upon a defendant's request, the government must permit the defendant to inspect and to copy or photograph books, papers, documents, data, photographs, tangible objects, buildings or places, or copies or portions of any of these items, if the item is within the government's possession, custody, or control and:

(i) the item is material to preparing the defense;

(ii) the government intends to use the item in its case-in-chief at trial; or

(iii) the item was obtained from or belongs to the defendant.

(F) Reports of Examinations and Tests. Upon a defendant's request, the government must permit a defendant to inspect and to copy or photograph the results or reports of any physical or mental examination and of any scientific test or experiment if:

(i) the item is within the government's possession, custody, or control;

(ii) the attorney for the government knows—or through due diligence could know—that the item exists; and

(iii) the item is material to preparing the defense or the government intends to use the item in its case-in-chief at trial.

(G) Expert witnesses. At the defendant's request, the government must give to the defendant a written summary of any testimony that the government intends to use under Rules 702, 703, or 705 of the Federal Rules of Evidence during its case-in-chief at trial. If the government requests discovery under subdivision (b)(1)(C)(ii) and the defendant complies, the government must, at the defendant's request, give to the defendant a written summary of testimony that the government intends to use under Rules 702, 703, or 705 of the Federal Rules of Evidence as evidence at trial on the issue of the defendant's mental condition. The summary provided under this subparagraph must describe the witness's opinions, the bases and reasons for those opinions, and the witness's qualifications.

(2)   Information Not Subject to Disclosure.

Except as Rule 16(a)(1) provides otherwise, this rule does not authorize the discovery or inspection of reports, memoranda, or other internal government documents made by an attorney for the government or other government agent in connection with investigating or prosecuting the case. Nor does this rule authorize the discovery or inspection of statements made by prospective government witnesses except as provided in 18 U.S.C. §3500.

(3)   Grand Jury Transcripts.

This rule does not apply to the discovery or inspection of a grand jury's recorded proceedings, except as provided in Rules 6, 12(h), 16(a)(1), and 26.2.

(b)   Defendant's Disclosure.

(1)   Information Subject to Disclosure.

(A) Documents and Objects. If a defendant requests disclosure under Rule 16(a)(1)(E) and the government complies, then the defendant must permit the government, upon request, to inspect and to copy or photograph books, papers, documents, data, photographs, tangible objects, buildings or places, or copies or portions of any of these items if:

(i) the item is within the defendant's possession, custody, or control; and

(ii) the defendant intends to use the item in the defendant's case-in-chief at trial.

(B) Reports of Examinations and Tests. If a defendant requests disclosure under Rule 16(a)(1)(F) and the government complies, the defendant must permit the government, upon request, to inspect and to copy or photograph the results or reports of any physical or mental examination and of any scientific test or experiment if:

(i) the item is within the defendant's possession, custody, or control; and

(ii) the defendant intends to use the item in the defendant's case-in-chief at trial, or intends to call the witness who prepared the report and the report relates to the witness's testimony.

(C) Expert witnesses.—The defendant must, at the government's request, give to the government a written summary of any testimony that the defendant intends to use under Rules 702, 703, or 705 of the Federal Rules of Evidence as evidence at trial, if—

(i) the defendant requests disclosure under subdivision (a)(1)(G) and the government complies; or

(ii) the defendant has given notice under Rule 12.2(b) of an intent to present expert testimony on the defendant's mental condition.

This summary must describe the witness's opinions, the bases and reasons for those opinions, and the witness's qualifications.

(2)   Information Not Subject to Disclosure.

Except for scientific or medical reports, Rule 16(b)(1) does not authorize discovery or inspection of:

(A) reports, memoranda, or other documents made by the defendant, or the defendant's attorney or agent, during the case's investigation or defense; or

(B) a statement made to the defendant, or the defendant's attorney or agent, by:

(i) the defendant;

(ii) a government or defense witness; or

(iii) a prospective government or defense witness.

(c)   *Continuing Duty to Disclose.*

A party who discovers additional evidence or material before or during trial must promptly disclose its existence to the other party or the court if:

(1) the evidence or material is subject to discovery or inspection under this rule; and

(2) the other party previously requested, or the court ordered, its production.

(d) Regulating Discovery.

(1)   Protective and Modifying Orders.

At any time the court may, for good cause, deny, restrict, or defer discovery or inspection, or grant other appropriate relief. The court may permit a party to show good cause by a written statement that the court will inspect ex parte. If relief is granted, the court must preserve the entire text of the party's statement under seal.

(2)   Failure to Comply.

If a party fails to comply with this rule, the court may:

(**A**) order that party to permit the discovery or inspection; specify its time, place, and manner; and prescribe other just terms and conditions;

(**B**) grant a continuance;

(**C**) prohibit that party from introducing the undisclosed evidence; or

(**D**) enter any other order that is just under the circumstances.

Rule 23.   Jury or Nonjury Trial

(a) Jury Trial.

If the defendant is entitled to a jury trial, the trial must be by jury unless:

(**1**) the defendant waives a jury trial in writing;

(**2**) the government consents; and

(**3**) the court approves.

(b) Jury Size.

(1)   In General.

A jury consists of 12 persons unless this rule provides otherwise.

(2)   Stipulation for a Smaller Jury.

At any time before the verdict, the parties may, with the court's approval, stipulate in writing that:

(**A**) the jury may consist of fewer than 12 persons; or

(**B**) a jury of fewer than 12 persons may return a verdict if the court finds it necessary to excuse a juror for good cause after the trial begins.

(3)   Court Order for a Jury of 11.

After the jury has retired to deliberate, the court may permit a jury of 11 persons to return a verdict, even without a stipulation by the parties, if the court finds good cause to excuse a juror.

(c)   *Nonjury Trial.*

In a case tried without a jury, the court must find the defendant guilty or not guilty. If a party requests before the finding of guilty or not guilty, the court must state its specific findings of fact in open court or in a written decision or opinion.

Rule 26.2.   Producing a Witness's Statement

(a)   *Motion to Produce.*

After a witness other than the defendant has testified on direct examination, the court, on motion of a party who did not call the witness, must order an attorney for the government or the defendant and the defendant's attorney to produce, for the examination and use of the moving party, any statement of the witness that is in their possession and that relates to the subject matter of the witness's testimony.

Rule 41.   Search and Seizure

(a)   *Scope and Definitions.*

(1)   Scope.

This rule does not modify any statute regulating search or seizure, or the issuance and execution of a search warrant in special circumstances.

(2)   Definitions.

The following definitions apply under this rule:

(**A**) "Property" includes documents, books, papers, any other tangible objects, and information.

(**B**) "Daytime" means the hours between 6:00 a.m. and 10:00 p.m. according to local time.

(**C**) "Federal law enforcement officer" means a government agent (other than an attorney for the government) who is engaged in enforcing the criminal laws and is within any category of officers authorized by the Attorney General to request a search warrant.

(**D**) "Domestic terrorism" and "international terrorism" have the meanings set out in 18 U.S.C. §2331.

(**E**) "Tracking device" has the meaning set out in 18 U.S.C. §3117(b).

(b)   Authority to Issue a Warrant.

At the request of a federal law enforcement officer or an attorney for the government:

(1) a magistrate judge with authority in the district—or if none is reasonably available, a judge of a state court of record in the district—has authority to issue a warrant to search for and seize a person or property located within the district;

(2) a magistrate judge with authority in the district has authority to issue a warrant for a person or property outside the district if the person or property is located within the district when the warrant is issued but might move or be moved outside the district before the warrant is executed;

(3) a magistrate judge—in an investigation of domestic terrorism or international terrorism—with authority in any district in which activities related to the terrorism may have occurred has authority to issue a warrant for a person or property within or outside that district; and

(4) a magistrate judge with authority in the district has authority to issue a warrant to install within the district a tracking device; the warrant may authorize

use of the device to track the movement of a person or property located within the district, outside the district, or both.

(c)   Persons or Property Subject to Search or Seizure.

A warrant may be issued for any of the following:

(1) evidence of a crime;

(2) contraband, fruits of crime, or other items illegally possessed;

(3) property designed for use, intended for use, or used in committing a crime; or

(4) a person to be arrested or a person who is unlawfully restrained.

(d)   Obtaining a Warrant.

(1)   In General.

After receiving an affidavit or other information, a magistrate judge—or if authorized by Rule 41(b), a judge of a state court of record—must issue the warrant if there is probable cause to search for and seize a person or property or to install and use a tracking device.

(2)   Requesting a Warrant in the Presence of a Judge.

(A) In General. A magistrate judge may issue a warrant based on information communicated by telephone or other reliable electronic means.

(B) Recording Testimony. Upon learning that an applicant is requesting a warrant under Rule 41(d)(3)(A), a magistrate judge must:

(i) place under oath the applicant and any person on whose testimony the application is based; and

(ii) make a verbatim record of the conversation with a suitable recording device, if available, or by a court reporter, or in writing.

(C) Recording Testimony. Testimony taken in support of a warrant must be recorded by a court reporter or by a suitable recording device, and the judge must file the transcript or recording with the clerk, along with any affidavit.

(3)   Requesting a Warrant by Telephonic or Other Means.

(A) In General. A magistrate judge may issue a warrant based on information communicated by telephone or other appropriate means, including facsimile transmission.

(B) Recording Testimony. Upon learning that an applicant is requesting a warrant, a magistrate judge must:

(i) place under oath the applicant and any person on whose testimony the application is based; and

(ii) make a verbatim record of the conversation with a suitable recording device, if available, or by a court reporter, or in writing.

(C) Certifying Testimony. The magistrate judge must have any recording or court reporter's notes transcribed, certify the transcription's accuracy, and file a copy of the record and the transcription with the clerk. Any written verbatim record must be signed by the magistrate judge and filed with the clerk.

(D) Suppression Limited. Absent a finding of bad faith, evidence obtained from a warrant issued under Rule 41(d)(3)(A) is not subject to suppression on the ground that issuing the warrant in that manner was unreasonable under the circumstances.

(e)   Issuing the Warrant.

(1)   In General.

The magistrate judge or a judge of a state court of record must issue the warrant to an officer authorized to execute it.

(2)   Contents of the Warrant.

(A) Warrant to Search for and Seize a Person or Property. Except for a tracking-device warrant, the warrant must identify the person or property to be searched, identify any person or property to be seized, and designate the magistrate judge to whom it must be returned. The warrant must command the officer to:

(i) execute the warrant within a specified time no longer than 14 days;

(ii) execute the warrant during the daytime, unless the judge for good cause expressly authorizes execution at another time; and

(iii) return the warrant to the magistrate judge designated in the warrant.

(B) Warrant Seeking Electronically Stored Information. A warrant under Rule 41(e)(2)(A) may authorize the seizure of electronic storage media or the seizure or copying of electronically stored information. Unless otherwise specified, the warrant authorizes a later review of the media or information consistent with the warrant. The time for executing the warrant in Rule 4(e)(2)(A) and (f)(1)(A) refers to the seizure or on-site copying of the media or information, and not to any later off-site copying or review.

(C) Warrant for a Tracking Device. A tracking-device warrant must identify the person or property to be tracked, designate the magistrate judge to whom it must be returned, and specify a reasonable length of time that the device may be used. The time must not exceed 45 days from the date the warrant was issued. The court may, for good cause, grant one or more extensions for a reasonable period not to exceed 45 days each. The warrant must command the officer to:

(i) complete any installation authorized by the warrant within a specified time no longer than 10 calendar days;

(ii) perform any installation authorized by the warrant during the daytime, unless the judge for good cause expressly authorizes installation at another time; and

(iii) return the warrant to the judge designated in the warrant.

(D) Return the warrant to the magistrate judge designated in the warrant.

(3)   Warrant by Telephonic or Other Means.

If a magistrate judge decides to proceed under Rule 41(d)(3)(A), the following additional procedures apply:

(A) Preparing a Proposed Duplicate Original Warrant. The applicant must prepare a "proposed duplicate original warrant" and must read or otherwise transmit the contents of that document verbatim to the magistrate judge.

(B) Preparing an Original Warrant. If the applicant reads the contents of the proposed duplicate original warrant, the magistrate judge must enter those contents into an original warrant. If the applicant transmits the contents by reliable electronic means, that transmission may serve as the original warrant.

(C) Modification. The magistrate judge may modify the original warrant. The judge must transmit any modified warrant to the applicant by reliable electronic means under Rule 41(e)(3)(D) or direct the applicant to modify the proposed duplicate original warrant accordingly.

(D) Signing the Warrant. Upon determining to issue the warrant, the magistrate judge must immediately sign the original warrant, enter on its face the exact date and time it is issued, and transmit it by reliable electronic means to the applicant or direct the applicant to sign the judge's name on the duplicate original warrant.

(f)   *Executing and Returning the Warrant.*

(1)   Warrant to Search for and Seize a Person or Property.

(A) Noting the Time. The officer executing the warrant must enter on it the exact date and time it was executed.

(B) Inventory. An officer present during the execution of the warrant must prepare and verify an inventory of any property seized. The officer must do so in the presence of another officer and the person from whom, or from whose premises, the property was taken. If either one is not present, the officer must prepare and verify the inventory in the presence of at least one other credible person. In a case involving the seizure of electronic storage media or the seizure or copying of electronically stored information, the inventory may be limited to describing the physical storage media that were seized or copied. The officer may retain a copy of the electronically stored information that was seized or copied.

(C) Receipt. The officer executing the warrant must give a copy of the warrant and a receipt for the property taken to the person from whom, or from whose premises, the property was taken or leave a copy of the warrant and receipt at the place where the officer took the property.

(D) Return. The officer executing the warrant must promptly return it—together with a copy of the inventory—to the magistrate judge designated on the warrant. The judge must, on request, give a copy of the inventory to the person from whom, or from whose premises, the property was taken and to the applicant for the warrant.

(2)   Warrant for a Tracking Device.

(A) Noting the Time. The officer executing a tracking-device warrant must enter on it the exact date and time the device was installed and the period during which it was used.

(B) Return. Within 10 calendar days after the use of the tracking device has ended, the officer executing the warrant must return it to the judge designated in the warrant.

(C) Service. Within 10 calendar days after the use of the tracking device has ended, the officer executing a tracking-device warrant must serve a copy of the warrant on the person who was tracked or whose property was tracked. Service may be accomplished by delivering a copy to the person who, or whose property, was tracked; or by leaving a copy at the person's residence or usual place of abode with an individual of suitable age and discretion who resides at that location and by mailing a copy to the person's last known address. Upon request of the government, the judge may delay notice as provided in Rule 41(f)(3).

(3)   Delayed Notice.

Upon the government's request, a magistrate judge—or if authorized by Rule 41(b), a judge of a state court of record—may delay any notice required by this rule if the delay is authorized by statute.

(4)   Return.

The officer executing the warrant must promptly return it—together with a copy of the inventory—to the magistrate judge designated on the warrant. The judge must, on request, give a copy of the inventory to the person from whom, or from whose premises, the property was taken and to the applicant for the warrant.

(g)   Motion to Return Property.

A person aggrieved by an unlawful search and seizure of property or by the deprivation of property may move for the property's return. The motion must be filed in the district where the property was seized. The court must receive evidence on any factual issue necessary to decide the motion. If it grants the motion, the court must return the property to the movant, but may impose reasonable conditions to protect access to the property and its use in later proceedings.

(h)   Motion to Suppress.

A defendant may move to suppress evidence in the court where the trial will occur, as Rule 12 provides.

(i)   *Forwarding Papers to the Clerk.*

The magistrate judge to whom the warrant is returned must attach to the warrant a copy of the return, of the inventory, and of all other related papers and must deliver them to the clerk in the district where the property was seized.

Excerpted Statutes

18 U.S.C.

§3142.   Release or Detention of a Defendant Pending Trial

(a) **In general.** —Upon the appearance before a judicial officer of a person charged with an offense, the judicial officer shall issue an order that, pending trial, the person be—

(1) released on personal recognizance or upon execution of an unsecured appearance bond, under subsection (b) of this section;

(2) released on a condition or combination of conditions under subsection (c) of this section;

(3) temporarily detained to permit revocation of conditional release, deportation, or exclusion under subsection (d) of this section; or

(4) detained under subsection (e) of this section.

(b) **Release on personal recognizance or unsecured appearance bond.** — The judicial officer shall order the pretrial release of the person on personal recognizance, or upon execution of an unsecured appearance bond in an amount specified by the court, subject to the condition that the person not commit a Federal, State, or local crime during the period of release and subject to the condition that the person cooperate in the collection of a DNA sample from the person if the collection of such a sample is authorized pursuant to section 3 of the DNA Analysis Backlog Elimination Act of 2000 (42 U.S.C. 14135a), unless the judicial officer determines that such release will not reasonably assure the appearance of the person as required or will endanger the safety of any other person or the community.

(c) **Release on conditions.** —(1) If the judicial officer determines that the release described in subsection (b) of this section will not reasonably assure the appearance of the person as required or will endanger the safety of any other person or the community, such judicial officer shall order the pretrial release of the person—

(A) subject to the condition that the person not commit a Federal, State, or local crime during the period of release and subject to the condition that the person cooperate in the collection of a DNA sample from the person if the collection of such a sample is authorized pursuant to section 3 of the DNA Analysis Backlog Elimination Act of 2000 (42 U.S.C. 14135a); and

(**B**) subject to the least restrictive further condition, or combination of conditions, that such judicial officer determines will reasonably assure the appearance of the person as required and the safety of any other person and the community, which may include the condition that the person—

(**i**) remain in the custody of a designated person, who agrees to assume supervision and to report any violation of a release condition to the court, if the designated person is able reasonably to assure the judicial officer that the person will appear as required and will not pose a danger to the safety of any other person or the community;

(**ii**) maintain employment, or, if unemployed, actively seek employment;

(**iii**) maintain or commence an educational program;

(**iv**) abide by specified restrictions on personal associations, place of abode, or travel;

(**v**) avoid all contact with an alleged victim of the crime and with a potential witness who may testify concerning the offense;

(**vi**) report on a regular basis to a designated law enforcement agency, pretrial services agency, or other agency;

(**vii**) comply with a specified curfew;

(**viii**) refrain from possessing a firearm, destructive device, or other dangerous weapon;

(**ix**) refrain from excessive use of alcohol, or any use of a narcotic drug or other controlled substance, as defined in section 102 of the Controlled Substances Act (21 U.S.C. 802), without a prescription by a licensed medical practitioner;

(**x**) undergo available medical, psychological, or psychiatric treatment, including treatment for drug or alcohol dependency, and remain in a specified institution if required for that purpose;

(**xi**) execute an agreement to forfeit upon failing to appear as required, property of a sufficient unencumbered value, including money, as is reasonably necessary to assure the appearance of the person as required, and shall provide the court with proof of ownership and the value of the property along with information regarding existing encumbrances as the judicial office may require;

(**xii**) execute a bail bond with solvent sureties; who will execute an agreement to forfeit in such amount as is reasonably necessary to assure appearance of the person as required and shall provide the court with information regarding the value of the assets and liabilities of the surety if other than an approved surety and the nature and extent of encumbrances against the surety's property; such surety shall have a net worth which shall have sufficient unencumbered value to pay the amount of the bail bond;

(xiii) return to custody for specified hours following release for employment, schooling, or other limited purposes; and

(xiv) satisfy any other condition that is reasonably necessary to assure the appearance of the person as required and to assure the safety of any other person and the community.

In any case that involves a minor victim [of selected crimes], a condition of electronic monitoring and each of the conditions specified at subparagraphs (iv), (v), (vi), (vii), and (viii).

(2) The judicial officer may not impose a financial condition that results in the pretrial detention of the person.

(3) The judicial officer may at any time amend the order to impose additional or different conditions of release.

(d) **Temporary detention to permit revocation of conditional release, deportation, or exclusion.**—If the judicial officer determines that—

(1) such person—

(A) is, and was at the time the offense was committed, on—

(i) release pending trial for a felony under Federal, State, or local law;

(ii) release pending imposition or execution of sentence, appeal of sentence or conviction, or completion of sentence, for any offense under Federal, State, or local law; or

(iii) probation or parole for any offense under Federal, State, or local law; or

(B) is not a citizen of the United States or lawfully admitted for permanent residence, as defined in section 101(a)(20) of the Immigration and Nationality Act (8 U.S.C. 1101(a)(20)); and

(2) such person may flee or pose a danger to any other person or the community;

such judicial officer shall order the detention of such person, for a period of not more than ten days, excluding Saturdays, Sundays, and holidays, and direct the attorney for the Government to notify the appropriate court, probation or parole official, or State or local law enforcement official, or the appropriate official of the Immigration and Naturalization Service. If the official fails or declines to take such person into custody during that period, such person shall be treated in accordance with the other provisions of this section, notwithstanding the applicability of other provisions of law governing release pending trial or deportation or exclusion proceedings. If temporary detention is sought under paragraph (1)(B) of this subsection, such person has the burden of proving to the court such person's United States citizenship or lawful admission for permanent residence.

(e) **Detention.**—If, after a hearing pursuant to the provisions of subsection (f) of this section, the judicial officer finds that no condition or combination of conditions will reasonably assure the appearance of the person as required and the safety of any other person and the community, such judicial officer shall order the detention of the person before trial. In a case described in subsection (f)(1) of this section, a rebuttable presumption arises that no condition or combination of conditions will reasonably assure the safety of any other person and the community if such judicial officer finds that—

(1) the person has been convicted of a Federal offense that is described in subsection (f)(1) of this section, or of a State or local offense that would have been an offense described in subsection (f)(1) of this section if a circumstance giving rise to Federal jurisdiction had existed;

(2) the offense described in paragraph (1) of this subsection was committed while the person was on release pending trial for a Federal, State, or local offense; and

(3) a period of not more than five years has elapsed since the date of conviction, or the release of the person from imprisonment, for the offense described in paragraph (1) of this subsection, whichever is later.

Subject to rebuttal by the person, it shall be presumed that no condition or combination of conditions will reasonably assure the appearance of the person as required and the safety of the community if the judicial officer finds that there is probable cause to believe that the person committed an offense for which a maximum term of imprisonment of ten years or more is prescribed in the Controlled Substances Act (21 U.S.C. 801 et seq.), the Controlled Substances Import and Export Act (21 U.S.C. 951 et seq.), or chapter 705 of title 46, an offense under section 924(c), 956(a), or 2332b of this title, or an offense listed in section 2332b(g)(5)(B) of title 18, United States Code, for which a maximum term of imprisonment of 10 years or more is prescribed or an offense involving a minor victim under [certain prescribed sections].

(f) **Detention hearing.**—The judicial officer shall hold a hearing to determine whether any condition or combination of conditions set forth in subsection (c) of this section will reasonably assure the appearance of such person as required and the safety of any other person and the community—

(1) upon motion of the attorney for the Government, in a case that involves—

(A) a crime of violence, or an offense listed in section 2332b(g)(5)(B) for which a maximum term of imprisonment of 10 years or more is prescribed;

(B) an offense for which the maximum sentence is life imprisonment or death;

(C) an offense for which a maximum term of imprisonment of ten years or more is prescribed in the Controlled Substances Act (21 U.S.C. 801 et seq.), the Controlled Substances Import and Export Act (21 U.S.C. 951 et seq.), or chapter 705 of title 46;

(D) any felony if such person has been convicted of two or more offenses described in subparagraphs (A) through (C) of this paragraph, or two or more State or local offenses that would have been offenses described in subparagraphs (A) through (C) of this paragraph if a circumstance giving rise to Federal jurisdiction had existed, or a combination of such offenses; or

(E) any felony that is not otherwise a crime of violence that involves a minor victim or that involves the possession or use of a firearm or destructive device (as those terms are defined in section 921), or any other dangerous weapon, or involves a failure to register under section 2250 of title 18, United States Code; or

(2) Upon motion of the attorney for the Government or upon the judicial officer's own motion, in a case that involves—

(A) a serious risk that such person will flee; or

(B) a serious risk that such person will obstruct or attempt to obstruct justice, or threaten, injure, or intimidate, or attempt to threaten, injure, or intimidate, a prospective witness or juror.

The hearing shall be held immediately upon the person's first appearance before the judicial officer unless that person, or the attorney for the Government, seeks a continuance. Except for good cause, a continuance on motion of such person may not exceed five days (not including any intermediate Saturday, Sunday, or legal holiday), and a continuance on motion of the attorney for the Government may not exceed three days (not including any intermediate Saturday, Sunday, or legal holiday). During a continuance, such person shall be detained, and the judicial officer, on motion of the attorney for the Government or sua sponte, may order that, while in custody, a person who appears to be a narcotics addict receive a medical examination to determine whether such person is an addict. At the hearing, such person has the right to be represented by counsel, and, if financially unable to obtain adequate representation, to have counsel appointed. The person shall be afforded an opportunity to testify, to present witnesses, to cross-examine witnesses who appear at the hearing, and to present information by proffer or otherwise. The rules concerning admissibility of evidence in criminal trials do not apply to the presentation and consideration of information at the hearing. The facts the judicial officer uses to support a finding pursuant to subsection (e) that no condition or combination of conditions will reasonably assure the safety of any other person and the community shall be supported by clear and convincing evidence. The person may be detained pending completion of the hearing. The hearing may be reopened, before or after a determination by the judicial officer, at any time before trial if the judicial officer finds that information exists that was not known to the movant at the time of the hearing and that has a material bearing on the issue whether there are conditions of release that will reasonably assure the appearance of such person as required and the safety of any other person and the community.

(g) **Factors to be considered.**— The judicial officer shall, in determining whether there are conditions of release that will reasonably assure the appearance of the person as required and the safety of any other person and the community, take into account the available information concerning —

(1) the nature and circumstances of the offense charged, including whether the offense is a crime of violence, a Federal crime of terrorism, or involves a minor victim or a controlled substance, firearm, explosive, or destructive device;

(2) the weight of the evidence against the person;

(3) the history and characteristics of the person, including —

(A) the person's character, physical and mental condition, family ties, employment, financial resources, length of residence in the community, community ties, past conduct, history relating to drug or alcohol abuse, criminal history, and record concerning appearance at court proceedings; and

(B) whether, at the time of the current offense or arrest, the person was on probation, on parole, or on other release pending trial, sentencing, appeal, or completion of sentence for an offense under Federal, State, or local law; and

(4) the nature and seriousness of the danger to any person or the community that would be posed by the person's release. In considering the conditions of release described in subsection (c)(1)(B)(xi) or (c)(1)(B)(xii) of this section, the judicial officer may upon his own motion, or shall upon the motion of the Government, conduct an inquiry into the source of the property to be designated for potential forfeiture or offered as collateral to secure a bond, and shall decline to accept the designation, or the use as collateral, of property that, because of its source, will not reasonably assure the appearance of the person as required.

(h) **Contents of release order.**—In a release order issued under subsection (b) or (c) of this section, the judicial officer shall —

(1) include a written statement that sets forth all the conditions to which the release is subject, in a manner sufficiently clear and specific to serve as a guide for the person's conduct; and

(2) advise the person of —

(A) the penalties for violating a condition of release, including the penalties for committing an offense while on pretrial release;

(B) the consequences of violating a condition of release, including the immediate issuance of a warrant for the person's arrest; and

(C) sections 1503 of this title (relating to intimidation of witnesses, jurors, and officers of the court), 1510 (relating to obstruction of criminal investigations), 1512 (tampering with a witness, victim, or an informant), and 1513 (retaliating against a witness, victim, or an informant).

(i) **Contents of detention order.**—In a detention order issued under subsection (e) of this section, the judicial officer shall —

(1) include written findings of fact and a written statement of the reasons for the detention;

(2) direct that the person be committed to the custody of the Attorney General for confinement in a corrections facility separate, to the extent practicable, from persons awaiting or serving sentences or being held in custody pending appeal;

(3) direct that the person be afforded reasonable opportunity for private consultation with counsel; and

(4) direct that, on order of a court of the United States or on request of an attorney for the Government, the person in charge of the corrections facility in which the person is confined deliver the person to a United States marshal for the purpose of an appearance in connection with a court proceeding.

The judicial officer may, by subsequent order, permit the temporary release of the person, in the custody of a United States marshal or another appropriate person, to the extent that the judicial officer determines such release to be necessary for preparation of the person's defense or for another compelling reason.

(j) **Presumption of innocence.**—Nothing in this section shall be construed as modifying or limiting the presumption of innocence.

§3144.   RELEASE OR DETENTION OF A MATERIAL WITNESS

If it appears from an affidavit filed by a party that the testimony of a person is material in a criminal proceeding, and if it is shown that it may become impracticable to secure the presence of the person by subpoena, a judicial officer may order the arrest of the person and treat the person in accordance with the provisions of section 3142 of this title. No material witness may be detained because of inability to comply with any condition of release if the testimony of such witness can adequately be secured by deposition, and if further detention is not necessary to prevent a failure of justice. Release of a material witness may be delayed for a reasonable period of time until the deposition of the witness can be taken pursuant to the Federal Rules of Criminal Procedure.

§3161.   TIME LIMITS AND EXCLUSIONS

(a) In any case involving a defendant charged with an offense, the appropriate judicial officer, at the earliest practicable time, shall, after consultation with the counsel for the defendant and the attorney for the Government, set the case for trial on a day certain, or list it for trial on a weekly or other short-term trial calendar at a place within the judicial district, so as to assure a speedy trial.

(b) Any information or indictment charging an individual with the commission of an offense shall be filed within thirty days from the date on which such individual was arrested or served with a summons in connection with such charges. If an individual has been charged with a felony in a district in which no grand jury has been in session during such thirty-day period, the period of time for filing of the indictment shall be extended an additional thirty days.

(c)(1) In any case in which a plea of not guilty is entered, the trial of a defendant charged in an information or indictment with the commission of an offense shall commence within seventy days from the filing date (and making public) of the information or indictment, or from the date the defendant has appeared before a judicial officer of the court in which such charge is pending, whichever date last occurs. If a defendant consents in writing to be tried before a magistrate judge on a complaint, the trial shall commence within seventy days from the date of such consent.

(2) Unless the defendant consents in writing to the contrary, the trial shall not commence less than thirty days from the date on which the defendant first appears through counsel or expressly waives counsel and elects to proceed pro se.

(d)(1) If any indictment or information is dismissed upon motion of the defendant, or any charge contained in a complaint filed against an individual is dismissed or otherwise dropped, and thereafter a complaint is filed against such defendant or individual charging him with the same offense or an offense based on the same conduct or arising from the same criminal episode, or an information or indictment is filed charging such defendant with the same offense or an offense based on the same conduct or arising from the same criminal episode, the provisions of subsections (b) and (c) of this section shall be applicable with respect to such subsequent complaint, indictment, or information, as the case may be.

(2) If the defendant is to be tried upon an indictment or information dismissed by a trial court and reinstated following an appeal, the trial shall commence within seventy days from the date the action occasioning the trial becomes final, except that the court retrying the case may extend the period for trial not to exceed one hundred and eighty days from the date the action occasioning the trial becomes final if the unavailability of witnesses or other factors resulting from the passage of time shall make trial within seventy days impractical. The periods of delay enumerated in section 3161(h) are excluded in computing the time limitations specified in this section. The sanctions of section 3162 apply to this subsection.

(e) If the defendant is to be tried again following a declaration by the trial judge of a mistrial or following an order of such judge for a new trial, the trial shall commence within seventy days from the date the action occasioning the retrial becomes final. If the defendant is to be tried again following an appeal or a collateral attack, the trial shall commence within seventy days from the date the action occasioning the retrial becomes final, except that the court retrying the case may extend the period for retrial not to exceed one hundred and eighty days from the date the action occasioning the retrial becomes final if unavailability of witnesses or other factors resulting from passage of time shall make trial within seventy days impractical. The periods of delay enumerated in section 3161(h) are excluded in computing the time limitations specified in this section. The sanctions of section 3162 apply to this subsection.

(f) Notwithstanding the provisions of subsection (b) of this section, for the first twelve-calendar-month period following the effective date of this section as set forth in section 3163(a) of this chapter the time limit imposed with respect to the period between arrest and indictment by subsection (b) of this section shall be sixty days, for the second such twelve-month period such time limit shall be forty-five days and for the third such period such time limit shall be thirty-five days.

(g) Notwithstanding the provisions of subsection (c) of this section, for the first twelve-calendar-month period following the effective date of this section as set forth in section 3163(b) of this chapter, the time limit with respect to the period between arraignment and trial imposed by subsection (c) of this section shall be one hundred and eighty days, for the second such twelve-month period such time limit shall be one hundred and twenty days, and for the third such period such time limit with respect to the period between arraignment and trial shall be eighty days.

(h) The following periods of delay shall be excluded in computing the time within which an information or an indictment must be filed, or in computing the time within which the trial of any such offense must commence:

(1) Any period of delay resulting from other proceedings concerning the defendant, including but not limited to—

(A) delay resulting from any proceeding, including any examinations, to determine the mental competency or physical capacity of the defendant;

(B) delay resulting from any proceeding, including any examination of the defendant, pursuant to section 2902 of title 28, United States Code;

(C) delay resulting from deferral of prosecution pursuant to section 2902 of title 28, United States Code;

(D) delay resulting from trial with respect to other charges against the defendant;

(E) delay resulting from any interlocutory appeal;

(F) delay resulting from any pretrial motion, from the filing of the motion through the conclusion of the hearing on, or other prompt disposition of, such motion;

(G) delay resulting from any proceeding relating to the transfer of a case or the removal of any defendant from another district under the Federal Rules of Criminal Procedure;

(H) delay resulting from transportation of any defendant from another district, or to and from places of examination or hospitalization, except that any time consumed in excess of ten days from the date an order of removal or an order directing such transportation, and the defendant's arrival at the destination shall be presumed to be unreasonable;

(I) delay resulting from consideration by the court of a proposed plea agreement to be entered into by the defendant and the attorney for the Government; and

(J) delay reasonably attributable to any period, not to exceed thirty days, during which any proceeding concerning the defendant is actually under advisement by the court.

(2) Any period of delay during which prosecution is deferred by the attorney for the Government pursuant to written agreement with the defendant, with the approval of the court, for the purpose of allowing the defendant to demonstrate his good conduct.

(3)(A) Any period of delay resulting from the absence or unavailability of the defendant or an essential witness.

(B) For purposes of subparagraph (A) of this paragraph, a defendant or an essential witness shall be considered absent when his whereabouts are unknown and, in addition, he is attempting to avoid apprehension or prosecution or his whereabouts cannot be determined by due diligence. For purposes of such subparagraph, a defendant or an essential witness shall be considered unavailable whenever his whereabouts are known but his presence for trial cannot be obtained by due diligence or he resists appearing at or being returned for trial.

(4) Any period of delay resulting from the fact that the defendant is mentally incompetent or physically unable to stand trial.

(5) Any period of delay resulting from the treatment of the defendant pursuant to section 2902 of title 28, United States Code.

(6) If the information or indictment is dismissed upon motion of the attorney for the Government and thereafter a charge is filed against the defendant for the same offense, or any offense required to be joined with that offense, any period of delay from the date the charge was dismissed to the date the time limitation would commence to run as to the subsequent charge had there been no previous charge.

(7) A reasonable period of delay when the defendant is joined for trial with a codefendant as to whom the time for trial has not run and no motion for severance has been granted.

(8)(A) Any period of delay resulting from a continuance granted by any judge on his own motion or at the request of the defendant or his counsel or at the request of the attorney for the Government, if the judge granted such continuance on the basis of his findings that the ends of justice served by taking such action outweigh the best interest of the public and the defendant in a speedy trial. No such period of delay resulting from a continuance granted by the court in accordance with this paragraph shall be excludable under this subsection unless the court sets forth, in the record of the case, either orally or in writing, its reasons for finding that the ends of justice served by the granting of such continuance outweigh the best interests of the public and the defendant in a speedy trial.

(B) The factors, among others, which a judge shall consider in determining whether to grant a continuance under subparagraph (A) of this paragraph in any case are as follows:

(i) Whether the failure to grant such a continuance in the proceeding would be likely to make a continuation of such proceeding impossible, or result in a miscarriage of justice.

(ii) Whether the case is so unusual or so complex, due to the number of defendants, the nature of the prosecution, or the existence of novel questions of fact or law, that it is unreasonable to expect adequate preparation for pretrial proceedings or for the trial itself within the time limits established by this section.

(iii) Whether, in a case in which arrest precedes indictment, delay in the filing of the indictment is caused because the arrest occurs at a time such that it is unreasonable to expect return and filing of the indictment within the period specified in section 3161(b), or because the facts upon which the grand jury must base its determination are unusual or complex.

(iv) Whether the failure to grant such a continuance in a case which, taken as a whole, is not so unusual or so complex as to fall within clause (ii), would deny the defendant reasonable time to obtain counsel, would unreasonably deny the defendant or the Government continuity of counsel, or would deny counsel for the defendant or the attorney for the Government the reasonable time necessary for effective preparation, taking into account the exercise of due diligence.

(C) No continuance under subparagraph (A) of this paragraph shall be granted because of general congestion of the court's calendar, or lack of diligent preparation or failure to obtain available witnesses on the part of the attorney for the Government.

(9) Any period of delay, not to exceed one year, ordered by a district court upon an application of a party and a finding by a preponderance of the evidence that an official request, as defined in section 3292 of this title, has been made for evidence of any such offense and that it reasonably appears, or reasonably appeared at the time the request was made, that such evidence is, or was, in such foreign country.

(i) If trial did not commence within the time limitation specified in section 3161 because the defendant had entered a plea of guilty or nolo contendere subsequently withdrawn to any or all charges in an indictment or information, the defendant shall be deemed indicted with respect to all charges therein contained within the meaning of section 3161, on the day the order permitting withdrawal of the plea becomes final.

(j)(1) If the attorney for the Government knows that a person charged with an offense is serving a term of imprisonment in any penal institution, he shall promptly—

(A) undertake to obtain the presence of the prisoner for trial; or

(B) cause a detainer to be filed with the person having custody of the prisoner and request him to so advise the prisoner and to advise the prisoner of his right to demand trial.

(2) If the person having custody of such prisoner receives a detainer, he shall promptly advise the prisoner of the charge and of the prisoner's right to demand trial. If at any time thereafter the prisoner informs the person having custody that he does demand trial, such person shall cause notice to that effect to be sent promptly to the attorney for the Government who caused the detainer to be filed.

(3) Upon receipt of such notice, the attorney for the Government shall promptly seek to obtain the presence of the prisoner for trial.

(4) When the person having custody of the prisoner receives from the attorney for the Government a properly supported request for temporary custody of such prisoner for trial, the prisoner shall be made available to that attorney for the Government (subject, in cases of interjurisdictional transfer, to any right of the prisoner to contest the legality of his delivery).

(k)(1) If the defendant is absent (as defined by subsection (h)(3)) on the day set for trial, and the defendant's subsequent appearance before the court on a bench warrant or other process or surrender to the court occurs more than 21 days after the day set for trial, the defendant shall be deemed to have first appeared before a judicial officer of the court in which the information or indictment is pending within the meaning of subsection (c) on the date of the defendant's subsequent appearance before the court.

(2) If the defendant is absent (as defined by subsection (h)(3)) on the day set for trial, and the defendant's subsequent appearance before the court on a bench warrant or other process or surrender to the court occurs not more than 21 days after the day set for trial, the time limit required by subsection (c), as extended by subsection (h), shall be further extended by 21 days.

28 U.S.C.

§2241. POWER TO GRANT WRIT

(a) Writs of habeas corpus may be granted by the Supreme Court, any justice thereof, the district courts and any circuit judge within their respective jurisdictions. The order of a circuit judge shall be entered in the records of the district court of the district wherein the restraint complained of is had.

(b) The Supreme Court, any justice thereof and any circuit judge may decline to entertain an application for a writ of habeas corpus and may transfer the application for hearing and determination to the district court having jurisdiction to entertain it.

(c) The writ of habeas corpus shall not extend to a prisoner unless

(1) He is in custody under or by color of the authority of the United States or is committed for trial before some court there of; or

(2) He is in custody for an act done or omitted in pursuance of an Act of Congress, or an order, process, judgment or decree of a court or judge of the United States; or

(3) He is in custody in violation of the constitution or laws or treaties of the United States; or

(4) He, being a citizen of a foreign state and domiciled therein is in custody for an act done or omitted under any alleged right, title, authority, privilege, protection, or exemption claimed under the commission, order or sanction of any foreign state, or under color thereof, the validity and effect of which depend upon the law of nations; or

(5) It is necessary to bring him into court to testify or for trial.

(d) Where an application for a writ of habeas corpus is made by a person in custody under the judgment and sentence of a court of a State which contains two or more Federal judicial districts, the application may be filed in the district court for the district wherein such person is in custody or in the district court for the district within which the State court was held which convicted and sentenced him and each of such district courts shall have concurrent jurisdiction to entertain the application. The district court for the district wherein such an application is filed in the exercise of its discretion and in furtherance of justice may transfer the application to the other district court for hearing and determination.

(e)(1) No court, justice, or judge shall have jurisdiction to hear or consider an application for a writ of habeas corpus filed by or on behalf of an alien detained by the United States who has been determined by the United States to have been properly detained as an enemy combatant or is awaiting such determination.

(2) Except as provided in paragraphs (2) and (3) of section 1005(e) of the Detainee Treatment Act of 2005 (10 U.S.C. 801 note), no court, justice, or judge shall have jurisdiction to hear or consider any other action against the United States or its agents relating to any aspect of the detention, transfer, treatment, trial, or conditions of confinement of an alien who is or was detained by the United States and has been determined by the United States to have been properly detained as an enemy combatant or is awaiting such determination.

§2242.   APPLICATION

Application for a writ of habeas corpus shall be in writing signed and verified by the person for whose relief it is intended or by someone acting in his behalf.

It shall allege the facts concerning the applicant's commitment or detention, the name of the person who has custody over him and by virtue of what claim or authority, if known.

It may be amended or supplemented as provided in the rules of procedure applicable to civil actions.

If addressed to the Supreme Court, a justice thereof or a circuit judge it shall state the reasons for not making application to the district court of the district in which the applicant is held.

§2243.   Issuance of Writ; Return; Hearing; Decision

A court, justice or judge entertaining an application for a writ of habeas corpus shall forthwith award the writ or issue an order directing the respondent to show cause why the writ should not be granted, unless it appears from the application that the applicant or person detained is not entitled thereto.

The writ, or order to show cause shall be directed to the person having custody of the person detained. It shall be returned within three days unless for good cause additional time, not exceeding twenty days, is allowed.

The person to whom the writ or order is directed shall make a return certifying the true cause of the detention.

When the writ or order is returned a day shall be set for hearing, not more than five days after the return unless for good cause additional time is allowed.

Unless the application for the writ and the return present only issues of law the person to whom the writ is directed shall be required to produce at the hearing the body of the person detained.

The applicant or the person detained may, under oath, deny any of the facts set forth in the return or allege any other material facts.

The return and all suggestions made against it may be amended, by leave of court, before or after being filed.

The court shall summarily hear and determine the facts, and dispose of the matter as law and justice require.

§2244.   Finality of Determination

(a) No circuit or district judge shall be required to entertain an application for a writ of habeas corpus to inquire into the detention of a person pursuant to a judgment of a court of the United States if it appears that the legality of such detention has been determined by a judge or court of the United States on a prior application for a writ of habeas corpus except as provided in section 2255.

(b)(1) A claim presented in a second or successive habeas corpus application under section 2254 that was presented in a prior application shall be dismissed.

(2) A claim presented in a second or successive habeas corpus application under section 2254 that was not presented in a prior application shall be dismissed unless—

(A) the applicant shows that the claim relies on a new rule of constitutional law, made retroactive to cases on collateral review by the Supreme Court, that was previously unavailable; or

(B)(i) the factual predicate for the claim could not have been discovered previously through the exercise of due diligence; and

(ii) the facts underlying the claim, if proven and viewed in light of the evidence as a whole, would be sufficient to establish by clear and convincing evidence that, but for constitutional error, no reasonable factfinder would have found the applicant guilty of the underlying offense.

(3)(A) Before a second or successive application permitted by this section is filed in the district court, the applicant shall move in the appropriate court of appeals for an order authorizing the district court to consider the application.

(B) A motion in the court of appeals for an order authorizing the district court to consider a second or successive application shall be determined by a three-judge panel of the court of appeals.

(C) The court of appeals may authorize the filing of a second or successive application only if it determines that the application makes a prima facie showing that the application satisfies the requirements of this subsection.

(D) The court of appeals shall grant or deny the authorization to file a second or successive application not later than 30 days after the filing of the motion.

(E) The grant or denial of an authorization by a court of appeals to file a second or successive application shall not be appealable and shall not be the subject of a petition for rehearing or for a writ of certiorari.

(4) A district court shall dismiss any claim presented in a second or successive application that the court of appeals has authorized to be filed unless the applicant shows that the claim satisfies the requirements of this section.

(c) In a habeas corpus proceeding brought in behalf of a person in custody pursuant to the judgment of a State court, a prior judgment of the Supreme Court of the United States on an appeal or review by a writ of certiorari at the instance of the prisoner of the decision of such State court, shall be conclusive as to all issues of fact or law with respect to an asserted denial of a Federal right which constitutes ground for discharge in a habeas corpus proceeding, actually adjudicated by the Supreme Court therein, unless the applicant for the writ of habeas corpus shall plead and the court shall find the existence of a material and controlling fact which did not appear in the record of the proceeding in the Supreme Court and the court shall further find that the applicant for the writ of habeas corpus could not have caused such fact to appear in such record by the exercise of reasonable diligence.

(d)(1) A 1-year period of limitation shall apply to an application for a writ of habeas corpus by a person in custody pursuant to the judgment of a State court. The limitation period shall run from the latest of—

(A) the date on which the judgment became final by the conclusion of direct review or the expiration of the time for seeking such review;

(B) the date on which the impediment to filing an application created by State action in violation of the Constitution or laws of the United States is removed, if the applicant was prevented from filing by such State action;

(C) the date on which the constitutional right asserted was initially recognized by the Supreme Court, if the right has been newly recognized by the Supreme Court and made retroactively applicable to cases on collateral review; or

(D) the date on which the factual predicate of the claim or claims presented could have been discovered through the exercise of due diligence.

(2) The time during which a properly filed application for State post-conviction or other collateral review with respect to the pertinent judgment or claim is pending shall not be counted toward any period of limitation under this subsection.

§2245. CERTIFICATE OF TRIAL JUDGE ADMISSIBLE IN EVIDENCE

On the hearing of an application for a writ of habeas corpus to inquire into the legality of the detention of a person pursuant to a judgment the certificate of the judge who presided at the trial resulting in the judgment, setting forth the facts occurring at the trial, shall be admissible in evidence. Copies of the certificate shall be filed with the court in which the application is pending and in the court in which the trial took place.

§2246. EVIDENCE; DEPOSITIONS; AFFIDAVITS

On application for a writ of habeas corpus, evidence may be taken orally or by deposition, or, in the discretion of the judge, by affidavit. If affidavits are admitted any party shall have the right to propound written interrogatories to the affiants, or to file answering affidavits.

§2247. DOCUMENTARY EVIDENCE

On application for a writ of habeas corpus documentary evidence, transcripts of proceedings upon arraignment, plea and sentence and a transcript of the oral testimony introduced on any previous similar application by or in behalf of the same petitioner, shall be admissible in evidence.

§2248. RETURN OR ANSWER; CONCLUSIVENESS

The allegations of a return to the writ of habeas corpus or of an answer to an order to show cause in a habeas corpus proceeding, if not traversed, shall be accepted as true except to the extent that the judge finds from the evidence that they are not true.

§2249.   CERTIFIED COPIES OF INDICTMENT, PLEA AND JUDGMENT;
            OF RESPONDENT

On application for a writ of habeas corpus to inquire into the detention of any person pursuant to a judgment of a court of the United States, the respondent shall promptly file with the court certified copies of the indictment, plea of petitioner and the judgment, or such of them as may be material to the questions raised, if the petitioner fails to attach them to his petition, and same shall be attached to the return to the writ, or to the answer to the order to show cause.

§2250.   INDIGENT PETITIONER ENTITLED TO DOCUMENTS WITHOUT COST

If on any application for a writ of habeas corpus an order has been made permitting the petitioner to prosecute the application in forma pauperis, the clerk of any court of the United States shall furnish to the petitioner without cost certified copies of such documents or parts of the record on file in his office as may be required by order of the judge before whom the application is pending.

§2251.   STAY OF STATE COURT PROCEEDINGS

A justice or judge of the United States before whom a habeas corpus proceeding is pending, may, before final judgment or after final judgment of discharge, or pending appeal, stay any proceeding against the person detained in any State court or by or under the authority of any State for any matter involved in the habeas corpus proceeding.

After the granting of such a stay, any such proceeding in any State court or by or under the authority of any State shall be void. If no stay is granted, any such proceeding shall be as valid as if no habeas corpus proceedings or appeal were pending.

§2252.   NOTICE

Prior to the hearing of a habeas corpus proceeding in behalf of a person in custody of State officers or by virtue of State laws notice shall be served on the attorney general or other appropriate officer of such State as the justice or judge at the time of issuing the writ shall direct.

§2253.   APPEAL

(a) In a habeas corpus proceeding or a proceeding under section 2255 before a district judge, the final order shall be subject to review, on appeal, by the court of appeals for the circuit in which the proceeding is held.

(b) There shall be no right of appeal from a final order in a proceeding to test the validity of a warrant to remove to another district or place for commitment or trial a person charged with a criminal offense against the United States, or to test the validity of such person's detention pending removal proceedings.

(c)(1) Unless a circuit justice or judge issues a certificate of appeal-ability, an appeal may not be taken to the court of appeals from —

(A) the final order in a habeas corpus proceeding in which the detention complained of arises out of process issued by a State court; or

(B) the final order in a proceeding under section 2255.

(2) A certificate of appealability may issue under paragraph (1) only if the applicant has made a substantial showing of the denial of a constitutional right.

(3) The certificate of appealability under paragraph (1) shall indicate which specific issue or issues satisfy the showing required by paragraph (2).

§2254. STATE CUSTODY; REMEDIES IN STATE COURTS

(a) The Supreme Court, a Justice thereof, a circuit judge, or a district court shall entertain an application for a writ of habeas corpus in behalf of a person in custody pursuant to the judgment of a State court only on the ground that he is in custody in violation of the Constitution or laws or treaties of the United States.

(b)(1) An application for a writ of habeas corpus on behalf of a person in custody pursuant to the judgment of a State court shall not be granted unless it appears that—

(A) the applicant has exhausted the remedies available in the courts of the State; or

(B)(i) there is an absence of available State corrective process; or

(ii) circumstances exist that render such process ineffective to protect the rights of the applicant.

(2) An application for a writ of habeas corpus may be denied on the merits, notwithstanding the failure of the applicant to exhaust the remedies available in the courts of the State.

(3) A State shall not be deemed to have waived the exhaustion requirement or be estopped from reliance upon the requirement unless the State, through counsel, expressly waives the requirement.

(c) An applicant shall not be deemed to have exhausted the remedies available in the courts of the State, within the meaning of this section, if he has the right under the law of the State to raise, by any available procedure, the question presented.

(d) An application for a writ of habeas corpus on behalf of a person in custody pursuant to the judgment of a State court shall not be granted with respect to any claim that was adjudicated on the merits in State court proceedings unless the adjudication of the claim—

(1) resulted in a decision that was contrary to, or involved an unreasonable application of, clearly established Federal law, as determined by the Supreme Court of the United States; or

(2) resulted in a decision that was based on an unreasonable determination of the facts in light of the evidence presented in the State court proceeding.

(e)(1) In a proceeding instituted by an application for a writ of habeas corpus by a person in custody pursuant to the judgment of a State court, a determination of a factual issue made by a State court shall be presumed to be correct. The applicant shall have the burden of rebutting the presumption of correctness by clear and convincing evidence.

(2) If the applicant has failed to develop the factual basis of a claim in State court proceedings, the court shall not hold an evidentiary hearing on the claim unless the applicant shows that—

(A) the claim relies on

(i) a new rule of constitutional law, made retroactive to cases on collateral review by the Supreme Court, that was previously unavailable; or

(ii) a factual predicate that could not have been previously discovered through the exercise of due diligence; and

(B) the facts underlying the claim would be sufficient to establish by clear and convincing evidence that but for constitutional error, no reasonable factfinder would have found the applicant guilty of the underlying offense.

(f) If the applicant challenges the sufficiency of the evidence adduced in such State court proceeding to support the State court's determination of a factual issue made therein, the applicant, if able, shall produce that part of the record pertinent to a determination of the sufficiency of the evidence to support such determination. If the applicant, because of indigency or other reason is unable to produce such part of the record, then the State shall produce such part of the record and the Federal court shall direct the State to do so by order directed to an appropriate State official. If the State cannot provide such pertinent part of the record, then the court shall determine under the existing facts and circumstances what weight shall be given to the State court's factual determination.

(g) A copy of the official records of the State court, duly certified by the clerk of such court to be a true and correct copy of a finding, judicial opinion, or other reliable written indicia showing such a factual determination by the State court shall be admissible in the Federal court proceeding.

(h) Except as provided in section 408 of the Controlled Substances Act, in all proceedings brought under this section, and any subsequent proceedings on review, the court may appoint counsel for an applicant who is or becomes financially unable to afford counsel, except as provided by a rule promulgated by the Supreme Court pursuant to statutory authority. Appointment of counsel under this section shall be governed by section 3006A of title 18.

(i) The ineffectiveness or incompetence of counsel during Federal or State collateral post-conviction proceedings shall not be a ground for relief in a proceeding arising under section 2254.

§2255.   FEDERAL CUSTODY, REMEDIES ON MOTION ATTACKING SENTENCE

A prisoner in custody under sentence of a court established by Act of Congress claiming the right to be released upon the ground that the sentence was imposed in violation of the Constitution or laws of the United States, or that the court was without jurisdiction to impose such sentence, or that the sentence was in excess of the maximum authorized by law, or is otherwise subject to collateral attack, may move the court which imposed the sentence to vacate, set aside or correct the sentence.

Unless the motion and the files and records of the case conclusively show that the prisoner is entitled to no relief, the court shall cause notice thereof to be served upon the United States attorney, grant a prompt hearing thereon, determine the issues and make findings of fact and conclusions of law with respect thereto. If the court finds that the judgment was rendered without jurisdiction, or that the sentence imposed was not authorized by law or otherwise open to collateral attack, or that there has been such a denial or infringement of the constitutional rights of the prisoner as to render the judgment vulnerable to collateral attack, the court shall vacate and set the judgment aside and shall discharge the prisoner or resentence him or grant a new trial or correct the sentence as may appear appropriate.

A court may entertain and determine such motion without requiring the production of the prisoner at the hearing.

An appeal may be taken to the court of appeals from the order entered on the motion as from a final judgment on application for a writ of habeas corpus.

An application for a writ of habeas corpus in behalf of a prisoner who is authorized to apply for relief by motion pursuant to this section, shall not be entertained if it appears that the applicant has failed to apply for relief, by motion, to the court which sentenced him, or that such court has denied him relief, unless it also appears that the remedy by motion is inadequate or ineffective to test the legality of his detention.

A 1-year period of limitation shall apply to a motion under this section. The limitation period shall run from the latest of—

(1) the date on which the judgment of conviction becomes final;

(2) the date on which the impediment to making a motion created by governmental action in violation of the Constitution or laws of the United States is removed, if the movant was prevented from making a motion by such governmental action;

(3) the date on which the right asserted was initially recognized by the Supreme Court, if that right has been newly recognized by the Supreme Court and made retroactively applicable to cases on collateral review; or

(4) the date on which the facts supporting the claim or claims presented could have been discovered through the exercise of due diligence.

Except as provided in section 408 of the Controlled Substances Act, in all proceedings brought under this section, and any subsequent proceedings on review, the court may appoint counsel, except as provided by a rule promulgated by the Supreme Court pursuant to statutory authority. Appointment of counsel under this section shall be governed by section 3006A of title 18.

A second or successive motion must be certified as provided in section 2244 by a panel of the appropriate court of appeals to contain—

(1) newly discovered evidence that, if proven and viewed in light of the evidence as a whole, would be sufficient to establish by clear and convincing evidence that no reasonable factfinder would have found the movant guilty of the offense; or

(2) a new rule of constitutional law, made retroactive to cases on collateral review by the Supreme Court, that was previously unavailable.

§2261. PRISONERS IN STATE CUSTODY SUBJECT TO CAPITAL SENTENCE; APPOINTMENT OF COUNSEL; REQUIREMENT OF RULE OF COURT OR STATUTE; PROCEDURES FOR APPOINTMENT

(a) This chapter shall apply to cases arising under section 2254 brought by prisoners in State custody who are subject to a capital sentence. It shall apply only if the provisions of subsections (b) and (c) are satisfied.

(b) This chapter is applicable if a State establishes by statute, rule of its court of last resort, or by another agency authorized by State law, a mechanism for the appointment, compensation, and payment of reasonable litigation expenses of competent counsel in State post-conviction proceedings brought by indigent prisoners whose capital convictions and sentences have been upheld on direct appeal to the court of last resort in the State or have otherwise become final for State law purposes. The rule of court or statute must provide standards of competency for the appointment of such counsel.

(c) Any mechanism for the appointment, compensation, and reimbursement of counsel as provided in subsection (b) must offer counsel to all State prisoners under capital sentence and must provide for the entry of an order by a court of record—

(1) appointing one or more counsels to represent the prisoner upon a finding that the prisoner is indigent and accepted the offer or is unable competently to decide whether to accept or reject the offer;

(2) finding, after a hearing if necessary, that the prisoner rejected the offer of counsel and made the decision with an understanding of its legal consequences; or

(3) denying the appointment of counsel upon a finding that the prisoner is not indigent.

(d) No counsel appointed pursuant to subsections (b) and (c) to represent a State prisoner under capital sentence shall have previously represented the prisoner at trial or on direct appeal in the case for which the appointment is made unless the prisoner and counsel expressly request continued representation.

(e) The ineffectiveness or incompetence of counsel during State or Federal post-conviction proceedings in a capital case shall not be a ground for relief in a proceeding arising under section 2254. This limitation shall not preclude the appointment of different counsel, on the court's own motion or at the request of the prisoner, at any phase of State or Federal post-conviction proceedings on the basis of the ineffectiveness or incompetence of counsel in such proceedings.

§2262.   Mandatory Stay of Execution; Duration; Limits on Stays of Execution; Successive Petitions

(a) Upon the entry in the appropriate State court of record of an order under section 2261(c), a warrant or order setting an execution date for a State prisoner shall be stayed upon application to any court that would have jurisdiction over any proceedings filed under section 2254. The application shall recite that the State has invoked the post-conviction review procedures of this chapter and that the scheduled execution is subject to stay.

(b) A stay of execution granted pursuant to subsection (a) shall expire if—

(1) a State prisoner fails to file a habeas corpus application under section 2254 within the time required in section 2263;

(2) before a court of competent jurisdiction, in the presence of counsel, unless the prisoner has competently and knowingly waived such counsel, and after having been advised of the consequences, a State prisoner under capital sentence waives the right to pursue habeas corpus review under section 2254; or

(3) a State prisoner files a habeas corpus petition under section 2254 within the time required by section 2263 and fails to make a substantial showing of the denial of a Federal right or is denied relief in the district court or at any subsequent stage of review.

(c) If one of the conditions in subsection (b) has occurred, no Federal court thereafter shall have the authority to enter a stay of execution in the case, unless the court of appeals approves the filing of a second or successive application under section 2244(b).

§2263.   Filing of Habeas Corpus Application; Time Requirements; Tolling Rules

(a) Any application under this chapter for habeas corpus relief under section 2254 must be filed in the appropriate district court not later than 180 days after final State court affirmance of the conviction and sentence on direct review or the expiration of the time for seeking such review.

(b) The time requirements established by subsection (a) shall be tolled—

(1) from the date that a petition for certiorari is filed in the Supreme Court until the date of final disposition of the petition if a State prisoner files the petition to secure review by the Supreme Court of the affirmance of a

capital sentence on direct review by the court of last resort of the State or other final State court decision on direct review;

(2) from the date on which the first petition for post-conviction review or other collateral relief is filed until the final State court disposition of such petition; and

(3) during an additional period not to exceed 30 days, if—

(A) a motion for an extension of time is filed in the Federal district court that would have jurisdiction over the case upon the filing of a habeas corpus application under section 2254; and

(B) a showing of good cause is made for the failure to file the habeas corpus application within the time period established by this section.

§2264. Scope of Federal Review; District Court Adjudications

(a) Whenever a State prisoner under capital sentence files a petition for habeas corpus relief to which this chapter applies, the district court shall only consider a claim or claims that have been raised and decided on the merits in the State courts, unless the failure to raise the claim properly is—

(1) the result of State action in violation of the Constitution or laws of the United States;

(2) the result of the Supreme Court's recognition of a new Federal right that is made retroactively applicable; or

(3) based on a factual predicate that could not have been discovered through the exercise of due diligence in time to present the claim for State or Federal post-conviction review.

(b) Following review subject to subsections (a), (d), and (e) of section 2254, the court shall rule on the claims properly before it.

§2265. Application to State Unitary Review Procedure

(a) For purposes of this section, a "unitary review" procedure means a State procedure that authorizes a person under sentence of death to raise, in the course of direct review of the judgment, such claims as could be raised on collateral attack. This chapter shall apply, as provided in this section, in relation to a State unitary review procedure if the State establishes by rule of its court of last resort or by statute a mechanism for the appointment, compensation, and payment of reasonable litigation expenses of competent counsel in the unitary review proceedings, including expenses relating to the litigation of collateral claims in the proceedings. The rule of court or statute must provide standards of competency for the appointment of such counsel.

(b) To qualify under this section, a unitary review procedure must include an offer of counsel following trial for the purpose of representation on unitary review, and entry of an order, as provided in section 2261(c), concerning appointment of counsel or waiver or denial of appointment of counsel for that purpose. No counsel appointed to represent the prisoner in the unitary review proceedings shall have previously represented the prisoner at trial in the case for which the appointment is made unless the prisoner and counsel expressly request continued representation.

(c) Sections 2262, 2263, 2264, and 2266 shall apply in relation to cases involving a sentence of death from any State having a unitary review procedure that qualifies under this section. References to State "post-conviction review" and "direct review" in such sections shall be understood as referring to unitary review under the State procedure. The reference in section 2262(a) to "an order under section 2261(c)" shall be understood as referring to the post-trial order under subsection (b) concerning representation in the unitary review proceedings, but if a transcript of the trial proceedings is unavailable at the time of the filing of such an order in the appropriate State court, then the start of the 180-day limitation period under section 2263 shall be deferred until a transcript is made available to the prisoner or counsel of the prisoner.

§2266.   LIMITATION PERIODS FOR DETERMINING APPLICATIONS AND MOTIONS

(a) The adjudication of any application under section 2254 that is subject to this chapter, and the adjudication of any motion under section 2255 by a person under sentence of death, shall be given priority by the district court and by the court of appeals over all noncapital matters.

(b)(1)(A) A district court shall render a final determination and enter a final judgment on any application for a writ of habeas corpus brought under this chapter in a capital case not later than 180 days after the date on which the application is filed.

(B) A district court shall afford the parties at least 120 days in which to complete all actions, including the preparation of all pleadings and briefs, and if necessary, a hearing, prior to the submission of the case for decision.

(C)(i) A district court may delay for not more than one additional 30-day period beyond the period specified in subparagraph (A), the rendering of a determination of an application for a writ of habeas corpus if the court issues a written order making a finding, and stating the reasons for the finding, that the ends of justice that would be served by allowing the delay outweigh the best interests of the public and the applicant in a speedy disposition of the application.

(ii) The factors, among others, that a court shall consider in determining whether a delay in the disposition of an application is warranted are as follows:

(I) Whether the failure to allow the delay would be likely to result in a miscarriage of justice.

(II) Whether the case is so unusual or so complex, due to the number of defendants, the nature of the prosecution, or the existence of novel questions of fact or law, that it is unreasonable to expect adequate briefing within the time limitations established by subparagraph (A).

(III) Whether the failure to allow a delay in a case that, taken as a whole, is not so unusual or so complex as described in subclause (II), but would otherwise deny the applicant reasonable time to obtain counsel, would unreasonably deny the applicant or the government continuity of counsel, or would deny counsel for the applicant or the government the reasonable time necessary for effective preparation, taking into account the exercise of due diligence.

(iii) No delay in disposition shall be permissible because of general congestion of the court's calendar.

(iv) The court shall transmit a copy of any order issued under clause (i) to the Director of the Administrative Office of the United States Courts for inclusion in the report under paragraph (5).

(2) The time limitations under paragraph (1) shall apply to—

(A) an initial application for a writ of habeas corpus;

(B) any second or successive application for a writ of habeas corpus; and

(C) any redetermination of an application for a writ of habeas corpus following a remand by the court of appeals or the Supreme Court for further proceedings, in which case the limitation period shall run from the date the remand is ordered.

(3)(A) The time limitations under this section shall not be construed to entitle an applicant to a stay of execution, to which the applicant would otherwise not be entitled, for the purpose of litigating any application or appeal.

(B) No amendment to an application for a writ of habeas corpus under this chapter shall be permitted after the filing of the answer to the application, except on the grounds specified in section 2244(b).

(4)(A) The failure of a court to meet or comply with a time limitation under this section shall not be a ground for granting relief from a judgment of conviction or sentence.

(B) The State may enforce a time limitation under this section by petitioning for a writ of mandamus to the court of appeals. The court of appeals shall act on the petition for a writ of mandamus not later than 30 days after the filing of the petition.

(5)(A) The Administrative Office of United States Courts shall submit to Congress an annual report on the compliance by the district courts with the time limitations under this section.

(B) The report described in subparagraph (A) shall include copies of the orders submitted by the district courts under paragraph (1)(B)(iv).

(c)(1)(A) A court of appeals shall hear and render a final determination of any appeal of an order granting or denying, in whole or in part, an application brought under this chapter in a capital case not later than 120 days after the date on which the reply brief is filed, or if no reply brief is filed, not later than 120 days after the date on which the answering brief is filed.

(B)(i) A court of appeals shall decide whether to grant a petition for rehearing or other request for rehearing en banc not later than 30 days after the date on which the petition for rehearing is filed unless a responsive pleading is required, in which case the court shall decide whether to grant the petition not later than 30 days after the date on which the responsive pleading is filed.

(ii) If a petition for rehearing or rehearing en banc is granted, the court of appeals shall hear and render a final determination of appeal not later than 120 days after the date on which the order granting rehearing or rehearing en banc is entered.

(2) The time limitations under paragraph (1) shall apply to—

(A) an initial application for a writ of habeas corpus;

(B) any second or successive application for a writ of habeas corpus; and

(C) any redetermination of an application for a writ of habeas corpus or related appeal following a remand by the court of appeals en banc or the Supreme Court for further proceedings, in which case the limitation period shall run from the date the remand is ordered.

(3) The time limitations under this section shall not be construed to entitle an applicant to a stay of execution, to which the applicant would otherwise not be entitled, for the purpose of litigating any application or appeal.

(4)(A) The failure of a court to meet or comply with a time limitation under this section shall not be a ground for granting relief from a judgment of conviction or sentence.

(B) The State may enforce a time limitation under this section by applying for a writ of mandamus to the Supreme Court.

(5) The Administrative Office of United States Courts shall submit to Congress an annual report on the compliance by the courts of appeals with the time limitations under this section.